133

World Bank Discussion Papers

Letting Girls Learn

Promising Approaches in Primary and Secondary Education

Barbara Herz,
K. Subbarao,
Masooma Habib,
and Laura Raney

The World Bank
Washington, D.C.

First printing September 1991
Second printing May 1992

Discussion Papers present results of country analysis or research that is circulated to encourage discussion and comment within the development community. To present these results with the least possible delay, the typescript of this paper has not been prepared in accordance with the procedures appropriate to formal printed texts, and the World Bank accepts no responsibility for errors.

The complete backlist of publications from the World Bank is shown in the annual *Index of Publications*, which contains an alphabetical title list (with full ordering information) and indexes of subjects, authors, and countries and regions. The latest edition is available free of charge from the Publications Sales Unit, Department F, The World Bank, 1818 H Street, N.W., Washington, D.C. 20433, U.S.A., or from Publications, The World Bank, 66, avenue d'Iéna, 75116 Paris, France.

ISSN: 0259-210X

Barbara Herz is chief of the Women in Development Division of the World Bank's Population and Human Resources Department. K. Subbarao is an economist in, and Masooma Habib and Laura Raney are consultants to, that division.

Library of Congress Cataloging-in-Publication Data

Letting girls learn : promising approaches in primary and secondary
education / Barbara Herz ... [et al.].
p. cm. — (World Bank discussion papers ; 133)
Includes bibliographical references.
ISBN 0-8213-1937-X
1. Women—Education—Developing countries. I. Herz, Barbara
Knapp. II. Series.
LC2572.L48 1991
376'.9172'4—dc20 91-28588
CIP

ABSTRACT

The economic and social returns to education for women are substantial; the latter are on the whole probably greater than those for men. Education raises the productivity and earnings of both men and women. Educated parents have healthier children and, while the father has some influence on their health, the mother has far more. Educated mothers have more educated children. Educating women slows population growth by creating new economic opportunities that compete with childbearing and child care. Men, who spend less time with children, are less conscious of this tradeoff. Thus by educating its women, a country can reduce poverty, improve productivity, ease population pressure, and offer its children a better future. Yet, paradoxically, many countries invest less in educating women than they do in educating men.

The difficulty is that the benefits from female education may seem more distant or elusive than the benefits from male education to parents, who must decide to send children to school -- and who usually pay a cost (direct or opportunity) to do so even where education is supposedly free. Given the economics of poverty and the traditions prevailing in much of the world, from the parents' perspective -- though not from society's -- male education may understandably seem a better investment than female education. To create a stronger case for parents' sending their daughters to school, policy makers should recognize the costs and benefits from the parents' perspective. If parents incur greater costs to educate girls but society reaps greater gains, then governments ought to consider special measures and targeted subsidies to help girls attend school.

To help policy makers, this paper analyzes the benefits from female education (who gains and in what ways) and the constraints (direct and opportunity costs, reflecting economics and tradition). It then outlines promising approaches for increasing female education. The demand for female education can be strengthened gradually through economic and sectoral policies that increase the returns. But, this paper focuses on education policies, many of which could be adopted now, to lower the costs, improve the quality, and increase access to education in ways that will allow more girls to attend school. It reports evidence of effectiveness and gives examples, particularly from projects involving the World Bank. Especially in poor countries, projects succeed best when they include a "package approach" to address what are typically multiple and powerful constraints to female education. The paper calls for increased monitoring and testing the cost-effectiveness of the kind of innovative packages now being tried in several developing countries.

ACKNOWLEDGEMENTS

The authors would like to acknowledge major contributions from T. Paul Schultz (especially Chapter 2) and from Rosemary Bellew and Elizabeth King (especially Chapter 4). Adriaan Verspoor, Alan Berg, Joan Claffey, Ruth Kagia, Douglas Keare, Shahid Khandker, Mubina Kirmani, Catherine Kleynhoff, Kathryn Johnston, Marlaine Lockheed, John Middleton, Andrew Rogerson, Thomas Schmidt, Roger Slade, James Socknat, Maurizia Tovo, and Carolyn Winter provided useful suggestions. Benjamin Patterson processed the data, designed all figures and tables, and wrote the technical notes on data sources. John De New provided technical assistance on data retrieval and statistical analysis. Audrey Sloan prepared the text of the report. Ann Hamilton provided guidance and direction. Interested readers may wish to consult Women's Education in Developing Countries: A Review of Barriers, Benefits and Policy by Elizabeth M. King and M. Anne Hill (eds.) to be published soon by the World Bank. The authors also appreciate partial financial support from the Government of Norway, Ministry of Development Cooperation.

FOREWORD

In 1987 the World Bank launched a stronger and more focused initiative to integrate attention to women in development through its analytical work and lending. The rationale for any long-term effort by the World Bank is its potential contribution to economic growth and the reduction of poverty. The Bank's women in development initiative is no exception. Expanding women's opportunities, especially in ways that enhance their productivity and earning potential, will improve women's own well-being and contribute to better economic performance, reduction of poverty, and better family living conditions. Over time it will also help to slow population growth and promote environmental sustainability. Because social and cultural forces influence women's economic productivity, deliberate and thoughtful effort is required to involve women more effectively in the development process. The Bank believes that priority should go to five fields: education, reproductive health, agriculture, private entrepreneurship, and the wage labor force.

The Women in Development Division is preparing a series of papers suggesting ways to improve opportunities for women in specific sectors. This paper on education is part of the series. It is meant not only to guide the World Bank, but also to help people in governments, other development agencies, non-governmental organizations or other institutions to develop better strategies to assist women. The series complements other activities of the Women in Development Division and other offices in the Bank -- including country assessments, project evaluations, and research on poverty and women's productivity -- that also make efforts to help women more practical and effective.

Ann O. Hamilton
Director
Population and Human Resources Department

TABLE OF CONTENTS

Appendices and Annexes

Tables

Figures

Boxes

SUMMARY

i. The economic and social returns to education for women are substantial and on the whole probably greater than those for men. Yet, paradoxically, many countries invest less in educating women. This "gender gap" is widest in Africa, the Middle East, and South Asia. And while it applies to every age, it is particularly worrisome at the secondary school level, where the benefits are especially high.

ii. By the time countries achieve the per capita levels of gross national income (GNI) found in most of Europe or North America, female enrollment rates have risen and the gender gap has narrowed or closed. But up to a per capita GNI of $2,000, countries vary enormously in their approach to educating women. That approach can be significantly shaped by public policy. Policy makers who would see their country's women educated must first understand the precise costs and benefits of female education: who pays and who profits.

iii. The economic returns to schooling accrue first to the educated individual: education raises the productivity of men and women both at home and in the workplace. Whether they are wage workers or self-employed as farmers or entrepreneurs, educated men and women earn more and have greater labor mobility. Macroeconomic policies obviously are critical in expanding economic opportunities, but education permits individuals to respond more effectively to such opportunities. The economic returns to schooling (usually expressed as an estimated percentage increase in wages) are similar for women and men.

iv. Education for women has an even greater payoff socially. Educated parents have healthier children and, while the father has some influence on their health, the mother has far more. Educated mothers or fathers also have more educated children, and maternal education tends particularly to influence girls' education. Educating women also slows population growth. Education creates new opportunities for women that compete with childbearing and child care, so women tend to opt for smaller families. Men, who spend less time with children, are less conscious of this trade-off and may prefer larger families as their incomes rise. So, by educating its women, a country can reduce poverty, improve productivity, ease population pressure, and offer its children a better future. These returns justify greater investment in schooling for girls than most countries have made.

v. The problem is that this portrait of female education may look decidedly less attractive to those responsible for sending children to school. Even where education is in theory compulsory, the decision to educate or not to educate lies mainly with the youngsters' families. Parents weigh the net advantages of sending children to school against the net advantages of keeping them home. Given the economics of poverty and the traditions prevailing in much of the world, from the parents' perspective -- though not from society's -- male education may understandably be a better investment and female education a luxury they can ill afford. To create a more compelling case for parents' sending their daughters to schools, policy makers should recognize the costs and benefits from the parents' perspective.

Costs

vi. Schooling is never free and seldom inexpensive, even when government pays for much of it. Parents are expected to pay direct costs for school fees, books, clothing, and so on. They also incur opportunity costs because they lose their children's availability for chores and may even forfeit their children's wages. Girls usually perform <u>more</u> chores at home than boys do, typically fetching wood and water, caring for younger siblings, and helping with food production and preparation. Such help may be crucial to a poor family's survival because it permits parents -- especially mothers -- to bring in more income from jobs outside the home. Although exceptions can be found, families seldom depend so heavily on boys. When younger children fall ill, it is their older sisters, not their brothers, who drop out of school to care for them. As the family's income rises, its daughters are needed less at home.

vii. Because information on children's wages is scarce, most analysts use the wage rate of an uneducated adult to estimate the opportunity cost of a child's time in school. This practice may be reasonably accurate for girls. But it may inflate the costs of schooling for boys because girls tend to be better substitutes for their mothers than boys are for their fathers.

viii. In many countries, girls may also need special physical protection. In some traditional cultures, girls require much stricter supervision and more concealing clothes when they travel outside the home. Usually this costs money, and where cultural requirements are extensive and strictly enforced, expenditures may be high. But because it is hard to put a price on them, they are seldom included in calculations of the costs of schooling. The total costs of educating girls have thus been understated by analysts, and the costs of educating boys may be overstated. But parents, reckoning these costs more accurately, often conclude that they cannot afford to educate girls.

<u>Benefits</u>

ix. While the costs of schooling to parents are clear and immediate, the benefits often are not. Parents realize limited benefits from their children's education -- and, in some countries, less from daughters than from sons. Educated children earn higher wages, but that helps parents only if those children provide remittances or old-age support. Parents may be skeptical of their daughters' ability to get good jobs or income, because women often face discrimination in the labor market or cannot get the resources they need to be successful farmers or entrepreneurs. Or parents may feel weaker ties to daughters if they "marry out" of their natal families or if custom discourages parents from accepting remittances from daughters. The greatest beneficiaries of female schooling are probably the woman's own children -- the grandchildren of those who pay.

x. For many parents, therefore, the returns to a daughter's education are uncertain and remote. The returns to a son's education are more obvious and immediate. Thus parents are dissuaded from educating their daughters.

xi. A vicious cycle ensues: Girls are kept home to help the family subsist day to day. Uneducated, they cannot compete with boys for wages when they grow up. Women earn less, so education is provided mainly to boys. And so girls are kept home. Cultural traditions may reflect and reinforce economic realities.

<u>Promising Remedies</u>

xii. Over the past two decades, some developing countries have begun to break this cycle, providing more schooling for girls as well as boys. Other countries have moved far more slowly. Commitment to education varies enormously, and does not inevitably grow in proportion to per capita GNI. China, whose per capita GNI is $510, has 37 percent of its school-age girls and 50 percent of its boys enrolled in secondary schools, about the same as Bolivia ($350), Tunisia ($1,310), and Saudi Arabia ($6,200). On the other hand, Sri Lanka ($330), the Philippines ($620) and Malaysia ($1,700) have about two-thirds of boys and girls alike enrolled at the secondary level; Jamaica ($940) and Peru ($1,070) have almost reached this level.

xiii. Because public policy explains much of this variation, it is instructive to examine different countries' efforts. To build demand for schooling for girls, governments have taken measures that:

- **Increase the economic returns of educating girls.**

- **Lower the costs to parents of educating girls.** These include direct costs, opportunity costs, and costs associated with cultural demands.

- **Provide direct incentives** such as scholarships that make it more attractive to send girls to school than to keep them at home.

xiv. Some of these measures involve special subsidies for female education. These are economically justifiable because the parents who pay for the costs have little to gain but society benefits greatly from the presence of educated women.

xv. **Education policy is not the only vehicle for promoting girls' schooling.** This paper focuses on education policy, but it is important to note briefly the role of macroeconomic and other policies in reducing opportunity costs, increasing returns, and complementing education policies.

xvi. Ideally, macroeconomic policies guide economies toward more efficient growth suited to their resources. For countries long on labor but short on capital and other resources, efficient growth requires labor-intensive production. Logically, that means more jobs. Women, however, sometimes face special restrictions on their employment in the wage labor force or on their ability to run their own farms or other businesses. They may have more difficulty than men in gaining access to the information, resources, and even markets that they need to be productive. They may be concentrated in low-paying jobs because they are unequipped or perhaps not allowed to compete.

xvii. Evidence suggests that governmental action can help women improve their productivity and earnings. Such policies and programs -- which are beyond the scope of this paper -- will gradually raise the returns to and presumably increase the demand for female schooling. Precisely how this process works, and at what pace in different economic and social environments, are matters that require more study.

xviii. Some steps would clearly reduce the opportunity costs of female schooling and build demand for female education. When water and fuelwood are nearby, for instance, girls can spend less time on chores. Better household technology can reduce the time spent on cooking and other chores. Child care programs can free older girls to go to school. Public transportation can save time and ease parental concerns for girls' safety. Again, research is needed to explore the exact impact of different steps on female schooling.

xix. Finally, children who are hungry or ill cannot be expected to learn effectively, and in parts of the developing world girls are fed and cared for less than boys. The excessive mortality of girls in much of Asia is well documented. Programs to encourage equal treatment of girls and boys and measures to feed and help the most disadvantaged can give more girls the strength to attend school and learn.

Education Policies

xx. Education policies are the most direct means of reducing the costs of girls' schooling and thus persuading more parents to educate their daughters. School systems and curricula can be redesigned to meet families' economic and social needs and, by improving the quality of education, satisfy whatever limited demand may already exist. Then, as more girls enroll or stay on in school, female education may become more widely accepted.

xxi. The evidence of "what works" in education is less solid than might have been hoped, but the experience of the past two decades suggests some promising approaches. With the proviso that policies must be tailored to individual countries, the following measures deserve consideration:

- **Institute "awareness campaigns."** One promising and inexpensive technique is to enlist leaders from various fields to urge parents to send their daughters -- as well as their sons -- to school and to allow the girls to prepare their lessons at home. China's experience is encouraging.

- **Recruit more female teachers.** Where male-female contact is proscribed, as in much of South Asia or the Middle East, evidence suggests the presence of female teachers can draw more girls into the schools. The problem is that the same cultural constraints that require girls to be taught by women also make it hard to attract women to rural schools. One solution is to recruit women locally, if necessary by easing qualifications and providing training, housing, or transport.

- **Protect girls' privacy** in coeducational settings, by providing separate facilities such as lavatories or separate hours for using canteens. Separate boarding facilities, though costly, may increase girls' enrollment.

- **Consider separate schools for girls**, making sure that the quality of education (including mathematics and science) is adequate. In many countries, the additional cost of separating the sexes may not be much, particularly in fairly densely populated areas, and research shows girls' enrollment and performance often improve when they attend girls' schools.

- **Offer more flexible school schedules and hours** so that girls can combine schooling with chores. Indications are that this has been effective in China and India.

- **Allow girls who are mothers or pregnant to remain in or return to school.** This is being tried in several countries, including Nigeria.

- **Provide child care** at schools so that older sisters or young mothers can attend class. This is also being tried, but has not yet been evaluated.

- **Establish special scholarships, waive fees, or offer other financial incentives for girls.**

Such incentives, which may be essential in the poorest countries, must be carefully managed and often targeted. But reports from Bangladesh and Guatemala, among other countries, show that they work.

xxii. Other measures promote the enrollment of both boys and girls but may help girls more if parents are more reluctant to send their daughters to school:

- **Bring schools closer to homes**, perhaps by building more smaller schools, rather than a few large, central schools at a considerable distance from most homes. Obviously distance is a deterrent, more for girls than for boys. Several countries, including Bangladesh, Colombia, Morocco, and Pakistan are opting for smaller local schools.

- **Improve the quality and relevance of schooling** by, for example, clamping down on teacher absenteeism, improving teacher training, revamping curricula to focus on essentials (including mathematics and science), and providing textbooks that eliminate gender bias and show women in nontraditional roles. Such measures will improve women's productivity in the home as well as in the workplace. They will promote economic efficiency by allowing women a wider choice of occupations.

- **Reduce the direct costs of education for all children** by, for instance, reducing fees or issuing free textbooks. Evidence suggests such steps -- which in effect improve the quality of education -- do more to raise girls' enrollment than boys'.

- **Deepen community involvement** in the design and implementation of education policies and local schooling.

- **Make school compulsory**, if that is reasonably practical for the country concerned.

xxiii. Particularly in low-income countries, education projects have had little or no effect when they addressed only one or two constraints on girls' schooling. In many cases, what these projects omitted was any effort to reduce costs to parents. This was no accident. Such cost-reduction usually requires new subsidies, which can strain government budgets and prove hard to administer. Projects have also failed for lack of cultural sensitivity or community support.

xxiv. Projects have been more successful when they comprised a package of measures, including carefully designed subsidies, such as scholarships, to deal with parents' many concerns about educating their daughters. By involving the community, policy makers have helped ensure that interventions (especially subsidies) are designed and administered appropriately. These packages have apparently not suffered from the problems of "system overload" that commonly plague complex programs addressing several issues simultaneously. Or perhaps the failure to deal with multiple issues has proved more serious than the problems involved in tackling them.

xxv. Unfortunately, subsidies are needed most in those countries that can least afford them. However, steps to upgrade education for all children can increase the internal efficiency of the school system enough that the measures may pay for themselves. Research suggests that children perform better and so repeat less and drop out less at one-room schoolhouses, or other small community schools, than at larger, centralized schools. More practical curricula, better trained teachers, and less teacher absenteeism should help both boys and girls. Flexible schedules may permit double shifts or other arrangements that use facilities more intensively. Child care programs may inexpensively promote children's health and nutrition and allow women to get better-paying jobs; the result may be larger tax revenues and smaller families. In brief, the social dividends from greater economic efficiency, better health, and lower fertility may far exceed the costs of subsidizing schooling for girls.

Establishing a "Virtuous Cycle"

xxvi. Women who are educated can and do put their education to use. When they are allowed to do so, these women can compete with men and earn similar incomes. As women's earnings grow, so do the returns to female schooling. More girls enroll in school, health improves, fertility falls, and the next generation is equipped to fare even better. In short, success breeds success.

xxvii. The question is how to launch this felicitous cycle. Is it better to focus on education policy or on macroeconomic or other measures that raise the returns to schooling by improving women's earning power? How complementary are education and other policies that promote women's earnings? Research is limited and situations vary from country to country. Still, some themes emerge.

xxviii. In poor agrarian societies where women's economic prospects are severely limited, it may be especially important to demonstrate that women can earn more, by instituting policies and programs to improve their access to labor markets, information, and resources. Such programs, if they increase women's productivity, promote female education. Research shows that mothers who are educated and earning good wages are likelier to urge their daughters to go to school; indeed, they may emphasize their daughters' schooling more than their sons'. Research has also shown that, in homes where men and women both earn good incomes, boys and girls have similar responsibilities for chores.

xxix. In a sense, this is surprising. Women often rely on their daughters to do chores so that they can work. Thus, if the goal is to maximize the family's income in the short term, then an increase in the mother's wages might be expected to result in more chore time and less school time for the girl. However, raising a mother's wages evidently has other "income effects": the family demands more of goods and services generally, including education for girls. Moreover, as their earnings rise, mothers may invest in labor-saving devices, allowing girls more time for school.

xxx. Other changes are more hopeful still. As they get beyond day-to-day subsistence issues, families can take a longer-term perspective and set their sights higher for their children. The mother who is educated and brings home a good income may acquire more status in the family and so, in turn, may her daughters. Research is needed to explore these issues, especially in low-income areas where relatively few girls are in school, but the potential benefits of female education are great.

xxxi. In the meantime, it would make sense to consider education policies to cut the costs -- both direct and opportunity -- and improve the quality of girls' schooling; such policies should address traditional cultural requirements and restrictions as well. A top priority should be research that would model and test more precisely how innovative education policies and other policies that improve women's productivity can be combined to maximize female education at minimum cost.

World Bank Experience

xxxii. World Bank lending has helped develop what evidence there is on "what works" to improve female education. Earlier Bank-financed projects seldom addressed parents' multiple concerns, but recent projects have combined various schemes to do so, especially in some of the poorest areas.

xxxiii. In one new project in Bangladesh, for example, 60 percent of new teachers must be women, and the Bank helps to finance only their salaries. After qualifications were relaxed to help local recruitment, 150,000 women -- and 50,000 men -- applied for the 6,000 positions. In addition, the government has waived tuition for girls in upper primary school. Some tuition scholarships, amounting to about half the total costs parents incur to send daughters to school, have been offered at the secondary level. Textbooks are being revised to reduce gender stereotyping, and small primary "satellite schools," linked to larger central schools, are being built in local communities.

xxxiv. In Morocco, the government plans to build smaller middle schools, in greater numbers and closer to students' homes. Schools will have lavatories with separate facilities for girls, and 15 percent of the new middle schools will have boarding facilities. Scholarships for boarders will be provided, half of them reserved for girls (now only 10 percent of rural boarders). It will be important to evaluate the costs and effects of these innovative efforts.

Structure of This Paper

xxxv. Chapter 1 reviews trends in male and female primary and secondary enrollment, including the persistence of the "gender gap" despite rising per capita GNI. Chapter 2 covers the private economic and social returns to female schooling. Chapter 3 addresses the constraints on female education, both those imposed by families and those caused by the type of schooling offered. Chapter 4 suggests ways to enroll more girls in school, reviews the experience of more than 300 Bank-assisted and other education projects in countries with disparate economies and cultures, and recommends priorities for action.

CHAPTER 1. CHANGES IN ENROLLMENT AND GENDER PARITY

1.01 The first section of this chapter analyzes changes between 1965 and 1987 in female and male enrollments in primary and secondary school. The second section examines factors that may explain these changes, to identify the contribution of education policy.

Changes in Male and Female Enrollment

1.02 The gross enrollment rate is defined as the number of children enrolled in a level of education expressed as a percentage of the population of the age group for that level[1]. In 1965 gross enrollment rates for boys were low, and those for girls even lower (see figure 1.1). By 1987 enrollment rates in primary school had increased to about 100 percent in Latin America and East Asia, virtually closing the "gender gap" (the difference between male and female enrollment). But despite progress in South Asia and Sub-Saharan Africa, the gender gap in primary schools there remained large. In 1987 about four-fifths of school-age boys were enrolled compared to roughly three-fifths of the girls. In the Middle East and North Africa enrollment rates in 1987 were higher than in 1965, but the gender gap remained wide. Improvements in female enrollment between 1965 and 1987 were substantial but varied among regions. And in South Asia, progress slowed in the 1980s (see figure B-1 in Annex B).

Figure 1.1 Educational Progress in the Regions, 1965 & 1987

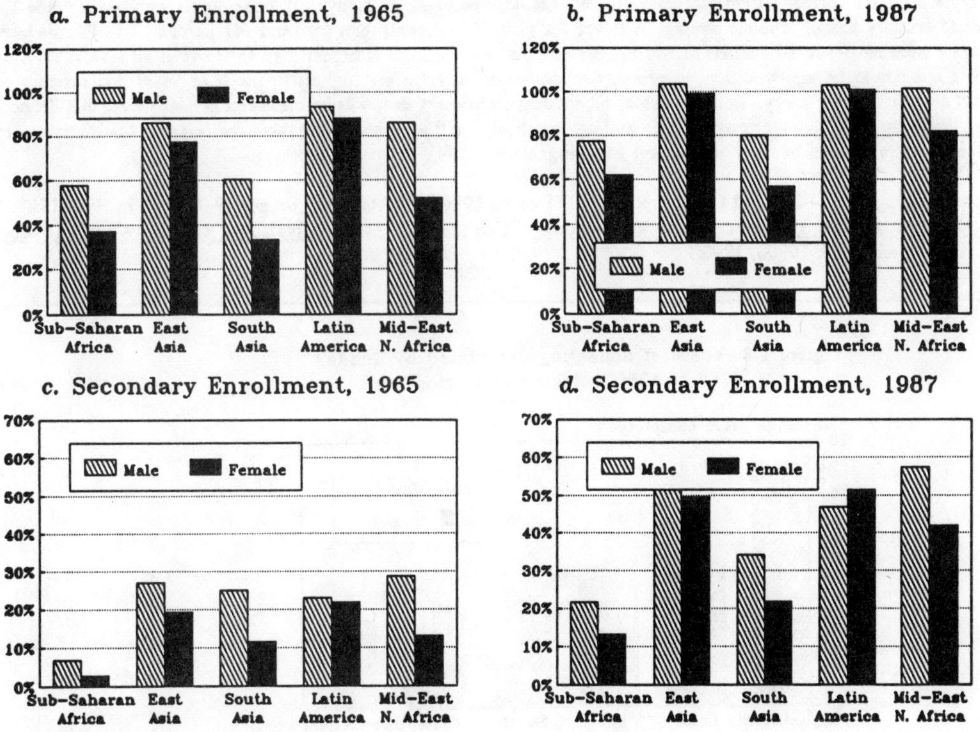

Source: See Annex A, Tables A-1 and A-2.

---

[1] For some countries the gross enrollment ratios may exceed 100% because some pupils are younger or older than the country's standard school age for that level.

1.03 Female enrollment rates rose faster in secondary schools than in primary schools. In Latin America and East Asia, about half the school-age boys and almost half the girls now attend school. In the Middle East and North Africa almost three-fifths of the boys but only two-fifths of the girls are enrolled. In Africa, despite a doubling of female enrollment since 1965, fewer than 15 percent of girls and 22 percent of boys attend secondary school. In South Asia about a third of the boys but only a fifth of the girls are enrolled. Girls' lower enrollment rates in secondary schools in Africa and South Asia reflect their earlier difficulties in primary schooling, as fewer girls are eligible to compete for places in secondary school. These low secondary enrollments also reflect the high rate of female dropouts (see box 1.1). Direct evidence on dropout rates is incomplete and unreliable, but Schultz (1989b) has compiled data on completed years of schooling, by region and by gender, that show the attainment rates of girls to be substantially lower than those of boys in South Asia, the Middle East, and Sub-Saharan Africa (see figure 1.2).

Box 1.1: Dropouts and Girls' Low School Attainment

Wastage -- dropouts and repetition -- is quite high in most developing countries: the proportion of students completing primary school in low-income countries is less than two-thirds and has fallen in recent years. (The World Bank classifies low-income countries as those having per capita incomes less than $450). Girls' dropout rates are generally higher than boys' in all regions. Wastage, which is associated with socioeconomic status, is highest in low-income countries. In 1988 the primary school dropout rate averaged 9.6 percent for girls but only 8.2 percent for boys in low-income countries; in middle-income countries, the rates were 6.1 percent and 5.9 percent, respectively. In Africa, girls' primary school dropout rates average 8.6 percent; boys' average 7.3 percent. The gender difference in dropouts from primary school is more pronounced in North Africa and the Middle East: 6.0 percent for girls compared to 4.3 percent for boys. In Latin America 7.8 percent of primary girls drop out and 8.8 percent of boys.

Country data clearly indicate the severity of the female dropout problem. Only 26.9 percent of girls in Malawi who enter first grade complete primary school; the corresponding percentage for boys is 45.9 percent. In Kenya, of those pupils who begin grade 1, fewer than half complete primary school, and the average is lower for girls (34 percent) than for boys (41 percent). In Bangladesh, only 5 percent of pupils entering Grade 1 complete Grade 12; the dropout rate for girls is higher than for boys at all levels. The dropout problem for girls appears to be age-specific: in primary schools dropout rates are highest in the later years and dropout rates in secondary school are particularly heavy. In the Gambia, recent data on primary dropouts by class and gender reveal that dropout rates for girls sharply increase in the later primary grades and are much higher than the dropout rates for boys. Most females drop out in grade 5, three-quarters of them because of marriage and pregnancy.

Sources: Bellew and King 1991; Lockheed and Verspoor 1991; Lycette 1986; Robertson and Berger 1986, cited in Hyde 1989; World Bank Bangladesh: Strategies for Enhancing the Role of Women, 1990; World Bank Kenya: The Role of Women in Economic Development, 1989; World Bank 1990b, 1990l.

Figure 1.2 Years of Schooling Completed by Gender (1960 to 1980, selected countries)

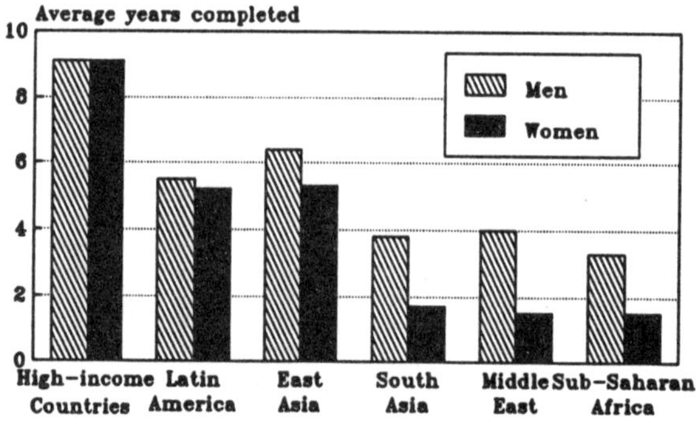

Note: Years of schooling completed reported in population censuses and surveys for various years between 1960 and 1980 for the age group 20-24. Adapted from Schultz 1989b, table 5

1.04 But regional averages tell only part of the story. Data for individual countries show that average enrollment rates and gender parity (the female/male student ratio) are only loosely related. Although parity improves as enrollment rises, there is no clearcut relationship (see figure 1.3). For example, some countries have reached gender parity in primary school at an average enrollment rate of about 60 percent, yet in several countries with primary enrollment rates above 80 percent, girls are still below parity with boys. Disparities are even greater at the secondary level.[2]

Figure 1.3 Total Average Enrollments and Gender Parity, 1987

a. Primary School

b. Secondary School

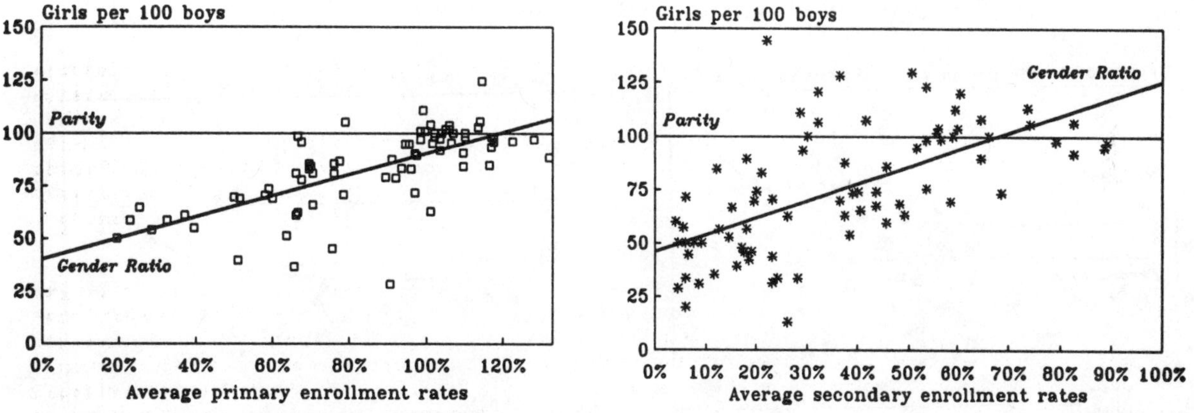

Source: see Annex A.

Progress in Schooling and Economic Growth

1.05 Education is a "normal" good: people demand more as their incomes grow. As per capita gross national income (GNI)[3] rises, school enrollment should also rise. This should hold true for both boys and girls. But in practice this process is neither fast nor automatic. Deliberate policy actions may be required, especially if higher female enrollments and gender parity are to be assured.

---

[2] The high ratio of girls to boys, especially in secondary schools, reflects in part the late entry of older students, high rates of repetition in some countries, and low levels of male enrollment (due, for example, to migration or war).

[3] Gross national income is defined as gross national product corrected for purchasing-power parity. Throughout this manuscript it is measured in constant U.S. 1980 dollars.

1.06 Figure 1.4 shows the dispersion in male and female enrollment rates and in parity (the female/male ratio) at primary and secondary levels for countries with per capita GNI up to $10,000 in 1987. Plotting the data on a log-linear scale allows a closer look at countries with per capita GNI between $100 and $1,000. Neither enrollment rates nor parity at the primary and secondary levels is more than loosely associated with per capita GNI. At low levels of per capita GNI, female enrollment rates and parity vary the most. Some low-income countries achieved high enrollment rates for all children; some wealthier countries -- particularly the oil exporters -- did so mainly for boys. Figures 1.5 and 1.6 compare primary and secondary enrollment and parity for 40 of the 77 countries plotted in figure 1.4 when ranked from lowest to highest per capita GNI. These figures demonstrate that enrollment rates and gender parity both vary for countries of similar per capita GNI.

Figure 1.4 Per Capita Income and Primary & Secondary Education, 1987

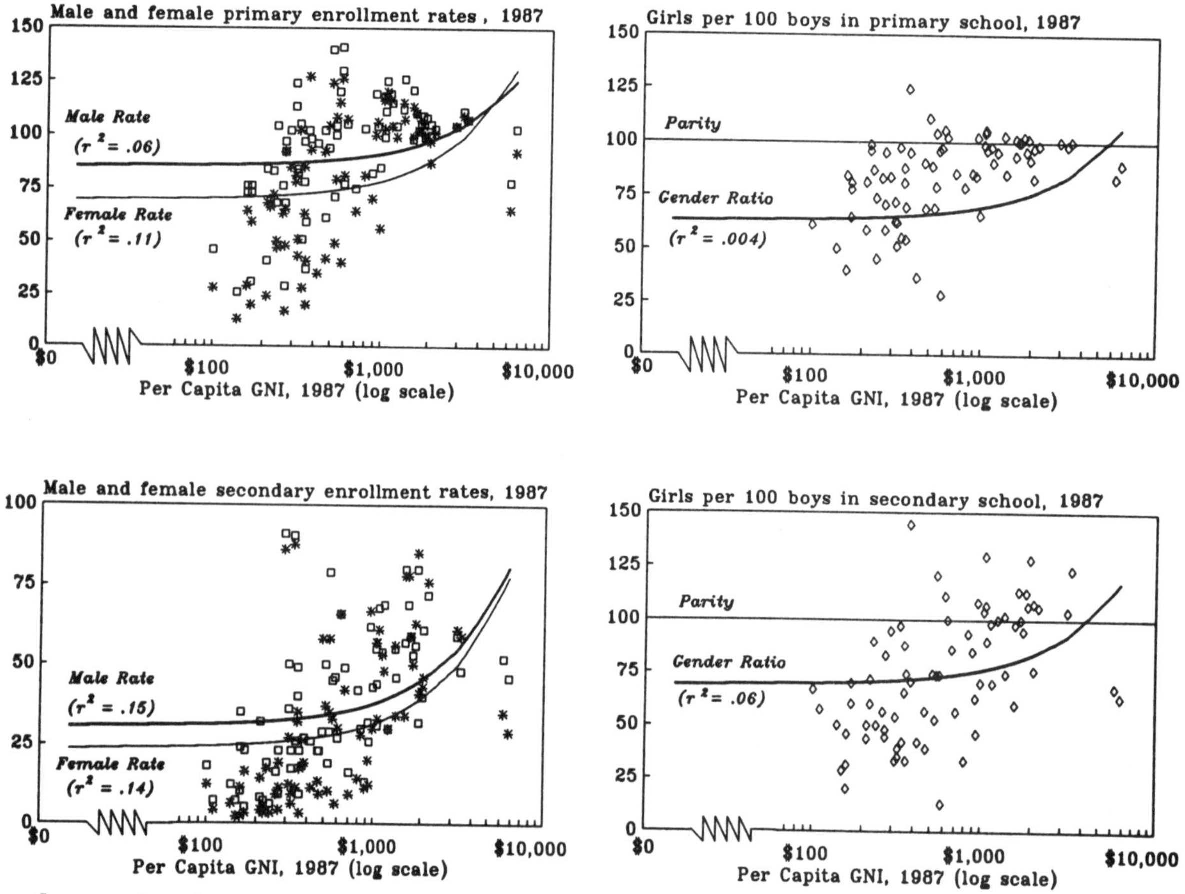

Source: see Annex A.

Figure 1.5 Female Share of Total Primary Enrollment Rate in Countries Ranked by Per Capita Income, 1987

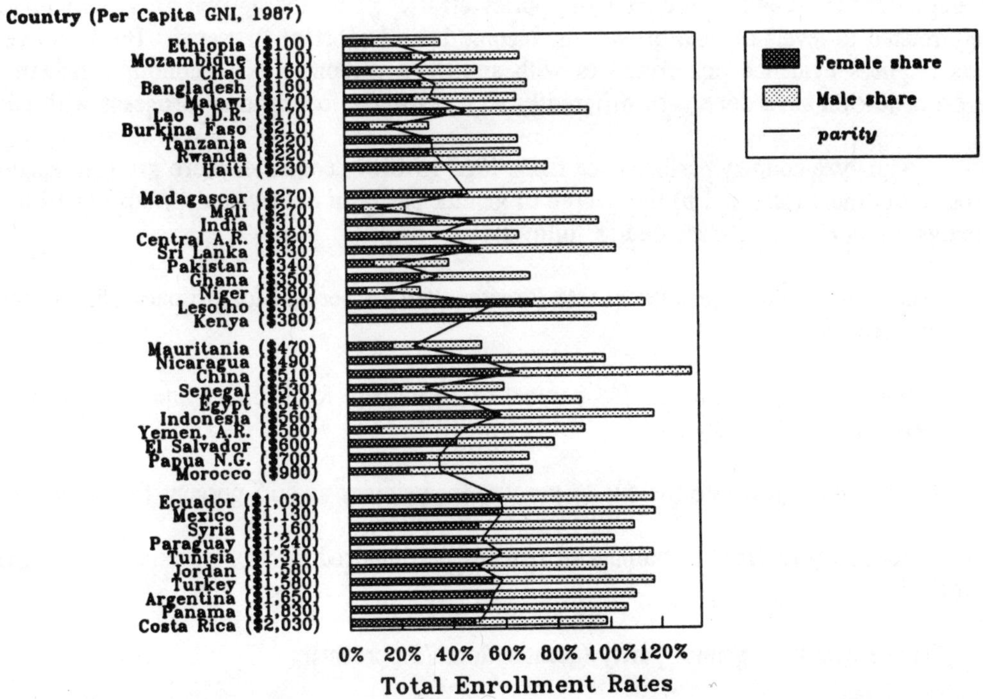

Figure 1.6 Female Share of Total Secondary Enrollment Rate in Countries Ranked by Per Capita Income, 1987

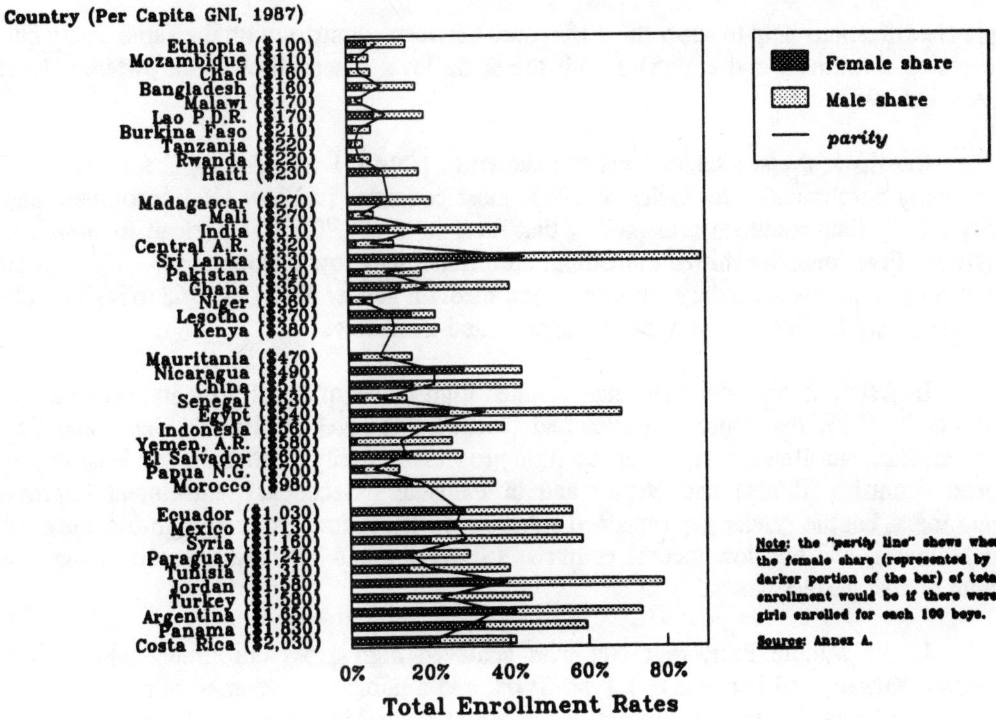

Note: the "parity line" shows where the female share (represented by the darker portion of the bar) of total enrollment would be if there were 100 girls enrolled for each 100 boys.

Source: Annex A.

1.07 Temporal progress in total enrollments together with gender parity may also depend on societal values and public policy. But it is difficult to prove the positive role played by policy; there are no good empirical measures of the effects of "policy effort." The finding that progress with parity is only loosely related to levels of, and growth in, income is an important first step. But to prove that policy matters requires evidence that countries with similar per capita GNI, economic growth, and expenditures on education have done very differently with respect to educational progress with parity.

1.08 To analyze country performance from 1965 to 1987, countries were grouped according to a) total gross enrollment rates and b) the degree of gender parity in both years. With regard to total gross enrollments, countries were classified as follows:

- Those with a high enrollment rate (greater than 75 percent for primary and 30 percent for secondary).
- Those with a medium rate (45 percent to 75 percent for primary and 16 percent to 30 percent for secondary).
- Those with a low rate (below 45 percent for primary and 15 percent for secondary).

Similarly, for gender parity (defined as number of females per hundred males), countries were grouped in three categories:

- Those with high gender parity (greater than 75 percent).
- Those with medium parity (45 percent to 75 percent).
- Those with low parity (below 45 percent).

These simple classifications help to show the differences between countries with the same parity but with different levels of enrollment and countries with the same level of enrollment but different levels of parity in 1965 and 1987.

1.09 Results at the secondary level are shown in table 1.1 (see Annex C for corresponding details for primary enrollment). In Africa in 1965, most countries had low total enrollment and low gender parity. Only four countries remained at that level in 1987: Central African Republic, Chad, Mali, and Niger. Five countries shifted to medium enrollment with low gender parity. Three countries made the transition from low secondary enrollment and medium gender parity in 1965 to high enrollment and high gender parity in 1987: Botswana, Mauritius, and Zimbabwe.

1.10 In Asia only two countries had attained high levels of enrollment in secondary school with near parity in 1965; two more countries had reached this level by 1987. Nepal and Pakistan progressed to medium enrollment rates but made little progress in parity. Progress was least impressive in the poorest countries (Bhutan and Nepal) and in Pakistan. Secondary enrollment improved in Indonesia and India, but the gender gap remained substantial. By contrast, in two high-income countries (Korea and Malaysia) and two low-income countries (Sri Lanka and Thailand), secondary enrollment expanded with almost perfect parity.[4]

1.11 In the Middle East, four countries achieved high gross enrollment and high parity (Algeria, Jordan, Kuwait, and Lebanon). Egypt, Syria, and a number of other countries progressed to higher average enrollment, but progress in parity was not as favorable. Afghanistan and Yemen lagged behind in both enrollment and parity.

---

[4] Most World Bank classifications include Pakistan in the Middle East and North Africa (EMENA). Here, Pakistan is placed in Asia.

Table 1.1: Transition Matrix for Changes in Secondary Enrollment and Gender Parity, from 1965 to 1987

Gender Ratio (girls per 100 boys)	Average Gross Enrollment Rates, 1965			Average Gross Enrollment Rates, 1987		
	LOW 1 - 15%	MEDIUM 16 - 30%	HIGH > 30%	LOW 1 - 15%	MEDIUM 16 - 30%	HIGH > 30%
Africa (n = 32)						
(HIGH) > 75	Lesotho				Lesotho Madagascar	Botswana Mauritius Zimbabwe
(MED.) 45 - 75	Mozambique Zimbabwe Botswana Burundi Mali Burkina Faso	Mauritius		Rwanda Ethiopia Tanzania Malawi Mozambique Uganda Burkina Faso Burundi Somalia	Kenya Cameroon Sudan Nigeria Zambia Sierra Leone Sengal Cote d'Ivoire	Ghana
(LOW) < 45	Nigeria Benin Madagascar Sierra Leone Liberia Ghana Tanzania Malawi Rwanda Ethiopia Kenya Uganda Senegal Zambia Sudan Zaire Somalia C.A.R. Cameroon Togo Cote d'Ivoire Mauritania Niger Chad			Mali C.A.R. Niger Chad	Zaire Liberia Mauritania Benin Togo	
Asia (n = 13)						
(HIGH) > 75			Philippines Sri Lanka		Thailand	Korea Sri Lanka Philippines Malaysia
(MED.) 45 - 75	Thailand Lao, PDR	Malaysia	Korea	Papua New Guinea	Lao, PDR Bangladesh	Indonesia India
(LOW) < 45	Indonesia Pakistan Nepal Bangladesh Papua New Guinea Bhutan	India		Bhutan	Pakistan Nepal	
The Middle East and North Africa (n = 15)						
(HIGH) > 75						Lebanon Jordan Kuwait Algeria
(MED.) 45 - 75	Algeria	Lebanon Iran	Kuwait	Afghanistan		Egypt Syria Tunisia Morocco Iran Saudi Arabia Iraq Turkey
(LOW) < 45	Morocco Yemen, PDR Afghanistan Saudi Arabia Yemen, Arab Rep.	Turkey Egypt Tunisia Iraq Syria	Jordan		Yemen, PDR Yemen, Arab Rep.	

Source: see Annex C

1.12 Two questions arise: which countries have expanded enrollments and improved parity and to what extent do the observed transitions correspond to levels of, and changes in, per capita income? A lack of correspondence would suggest that education policy may have played a role in any changes.

1.13 Countries were grouped according to three levels of performance in table 1.2: a) those with sustained progress in both gross enrollment and parity (**"best" performers**); b) those with moderate growth in enrollment and gradual improvement in parity (**"good" performers**); and c) those with low to moderate growth in enrollment and persistently low gender parity (**"worst" performers**). Are the "best," "good," and "worst" performing countries similarly placed in terms of levels of and growth in per capita GNI? If so, education policy must have played a role.[5]

1.14 Table 1.2 shows best, good, and worst performers spread widely across selected measures: per capita GNI, growth of per capita GNI, and level of public spending on education as a percent of GNI (see tables C-4, C-5, and C-6 in Annex C for distributions for both primary and secondary enrollment).

1.15 For example, countries with per capita GNI below $400 include best performers (Sri Lanka), good performers (India and Lesotho) and worst performers (Benin, C.A.R., Niger, Pakistan and Togo). Similarly, countries with a real change in per capita GNI of less than 70 percent between 1965 and 1987 include best, good, and worst performers. Even public spending per se is no guarantee of improved enrollment with parity: countries spending 2-4 percent of GNI (most countries) include best performers (Korea and Sri Lanka), good performers (Ghana and India) and worst performers (C.A.R., Liberia, Mali, and Mauritania).

1.16 To test these findings more rigorously, a series of ordinary least squares regressions (OLS) were run on a subset (39) of the 77 countries used in figure 1.3 for which data on certain variables were available. These regressions sought to explain total, male, and female gross enrollment rates, and gender parity as a function of adult male literacy, adult female literacy, per capita GNI the size of the economy's agricultural and service sectors, and spending on primary education, and on all education. We could not establish a significant positive relationship between female enrollment or gender parity and per capita GNI. But adult female literacy -- the result of past investments in female education -- had a powerful positive effect on both female and male enrollments and parity. Notwithstanding the small sample size and poor quality of the data, these findings conform to the arguments advanced in the previous paragraphs.

[5] The point is not to establish causality for the observed transition. The difficulty of demonstrating causality with international cross-section data are well known.

Table 1.2: Educational Growth with Equity (from 1965 to 1987) at the Secondary Level, Best, Good and Worst Performers Distributed by Income Levels, Income Growth and Expenditure on Education

a. Best, Good and Worst Performers and Per Capita Income Levels, 1987

Performance: Enrollment & Equity	Per Capita Income (in 1980 dollars), 1987 (n = 35)			
	< 400	400 - 699	700 - 1,000	> 1,000
Best	Sri Lanka	Zimbabwe Philippines		Korea Algeria Malaysia Mauritius Jordan Botswana
Good	Lesotho India Madagascar Bangladesh	Indonesia Egypt	Morocco Papua New Guinea Thailand	Turkey Tunisia Syria
Worst	Pakistan Benin C.A.R. Niger Togo Mali Zaire Chad Nepal Bhutan	Yemen, Arab Rep. Mauritania Yemen, PDR	Nigeria	

b. Best, Good and Worst Performers and Real Growth in Per Capita Income

Performance: Enrollment & Equity	Percent Change in Per Capita Income (in 1980 dollars), from 1968 to 1987 (n = 27)			
	< 20%	21% - 70%	71% - 100%	> 100%
Best		Philippines	Sri Lanka Malaysia	Korea Botswana Algeria Mauritius
Good	Ghana Madagascar	Morocco Egypt Turkey India	Lesotho Thailand Tunisia Syria	Indonesia
Worst	Zaire Chad Niger Mauritania Togo Benin C.A.R.	Mali Pakistan		

c. Best, Good and Worst Performers and Expenditure on Education

Performance: Enrollment & Equity	Expenditure on Education a Percent of GNP for 1975, 1980 and 1985 averaged (n = 29)			
	< 2%	2% - 3.9%	4% - 5.9%	> 6%
Best	Philippines	Sri Lanka Korea Kuwait	Mauritius	Botswana Algeria Zimbabwe Jordan Malaysia
Good		Ghana India Indonesia Turkey	Tunisia Egypt Syria Lesotho	Iran Morocco
Worst		Mauritania C.A.R. Liberia Mali Niger Nepal Pakistan	Togo	Yemen, AR

1.17 What conclusions can be drawn? First, neither high levels of per capita GNI nor economic growth ensures improved female enrollment with gender parity. Higher female enrollment rates and gender parity do not occur automatically as development proceeds. So waiting for per capita GNI to grow enough to "fix" the gender gap in education and raise female enrollment is not a promising strategy for most poor countries. Second, several countries with low per capita income and limited economic growth achieved remarkable improvements in female enrollment with gender parity. In these countries deliberate public policy choices evidently made a difference, and it was not simply a matter of increasing spending on education. One can understand what policy actions are needed only after identifying and understanding the returns to female education. These returns are examined in the next chapter.

CHAPTER 2. THE RETURNS TO FEMALE EDUCATION

2.01 The benefits from education accrue to individuals, families, and society. Individuals can expand their interests and skills and earn more income. The broader social benefits of education -- such as lower fertility, better health, and more education for the next generation[1] -- are harder to capture in economic terms. But the direct costs of education may be heavy -- as much as a third of government revenues and a tenth of household consumption in some cases -- and families and societies invest less in education for women than for men. This chapter compares the returns to investments in male and female education. It covers both the private economic returns to individuals and the broader social returns to families and societies and suggests why these may differ for men and women. It also outlines the conceptual issues involved in estimating returns to schooling and assesses the empirical evidence.

Private Economic Returns to Female Education

2.02 The private economic return on any investment is defined as the internal rate of return that equalizes the present discounted value of the stream of private benefits and the private cost to the investor. The private economic rate of return to education is usually defined as the rate that equates the costs to the student with the present discounted value of the increase in net income (less taxes) that the student will earn with an education. In estimating the private return, several assumptions are usually made:

a) Incomes are measured by wage rates because incomes of the self-employed are harder to assess, so that estimates of returns to schooling are confined to people in the wage labor force. The return to schooling is approximately the resulting percentage increase in the educated person's wage rate.

b) The private cost is assumed to be the opportunity cost of the student's time -- the student's foregone income. In principle this income should be valued at the prevailing wage rate for school-age children. But sometimes the market for children's labor is so limited that no reliable wage rate exists, or surveys neglect to ask about children's wages. Then analysts usually use the wage of adults without this education as a proxy for children's wages.

c) Other assumptions are also made to justify using particular estimation techniques, but these do not matter much for differentiating between men and women. For example, students' ability is routinely ignored for lack of data.

2.03 A wealth of research in the past twenty years has established that the private economic returns to schooling are substantial. Often the returns are highest for primary education, more moderate for secondary education, and lower (but still considerable) for higher education. More recent studies suggest that the returns on secondary education are now comparable to those for primary education. The returns to schooling for both men and women are considerable but the returns for women sometimes appear to be lower (see table 2.1).

---

[1] Schultz (1989a) contains detailed treatment of methodological issues, upon which this discussion of benefits draws heavily.

Table 2.1: Returns to Education by Gender and School Level: 1959-1985

Country (year of data)	Method of Estimation[a]	Primary Male	Primary Female	Secondary Male	Secondary Female	Higher Male	Higher Female
United States (1949)	I	17.8	5.6	14.0	13.0	9.7	4.2
Bogota, Colombia (1965)	II	18.2	nil	34.4	18.9	4.5	5.3
Germany (ca 1960)	b	..	..	..	..	4.6	5.0
Greece (ca 1960)	b	..	..	3.0	5.0	..	..
Kenya (ca 1960)	I	21.7	7.1	23.6	19.5	..	..
Malaysia (ca 1960)	b	9.4	9.3	12.3	11.4	10.7	9.8
New Zealand (ca 1960)	b	..	..	19.4	25.3	13.4	13.5
Brazil (1960)	b	17.9	38.5	..	..	..	..
Australia (ca 1960)	I	..	..	..	..	21.1	21.2
France (1976)	b	..	..	14.8	16.2	20.0	12.7
United Kingdom (1971)	b	..	..	10.0	8.0	8.0	12.0
Japan (1980)	I	..	..	..	..	5.7	5.8
South Korea (1971)	b	..	..	13.7	16.9	15.7	22.9
Taiwan (1982)	b	8.4	16.0	..	..	..	..
Puerto Rico (1959)	b	29.5	18.4	27.3	40.8	21.9	9.0
Andhra Pradesh, India (1977)	II	8.9	11.8	8.7	11.9	6.2	8.9
	I	7.2	.3	6.8	2.41	5.5	5.5
Ivory Coast (1985)	II	18.3	5.5	17.0	28.7	21.1	13.6

[a]Estimation Methods: I - use participation rate in labor force to deflate returns, depressing female returns disproportionately; II - estimate wage rate relationship without deflating by participation rates in the labor force.

[b]Estimation method not known.

** Not reported.

Source: Schultz 1989a.

2.04 These estimates of the returns to schooling may be misleading for several reasons. For one thing, only participants in the labor force are included. Many studies (noted with I in table 2.1) simply assume that people outside the wage labor force are unproductive and deflate the returns to education by the proportion of people in the wage labor force. Since a smaller proportion of women than men participate in the labor force, this procedure gives the impression that returns to education are higher for men than for women. A study from Andhra Pradesh, India, illustrates the effect of this procedure. The returns for women fall from about 12 percent to 0.3 percent for the primary level, and from 12 percent to 2.4 percent for the secondary level, when deflated by participation rates in the labor force.

2.05 But Schultz (1986a) and others argue that women (or men) who do not work in the wage labor force may remain outside of it by choice. Logic suggests that people should weigh their options and join the wage labor force only if they think they can be more productive there than outside it, working as farmers, entrepreneurs, or home-based workers. Women who have access to land, for example, may prefer to farm. People who choose to join the wage labor force are self-selected and this selection bias has implications for how to measure the returns to schooling.

2.06 The returns to education will be underestimated if they are deflated by labor force participation rates based on the mistaken assumption that people are not productive outside the labor force. They will also be wrong if they fail to correct for the selection bias. Since fewer women join the labor force, the bias is likely to matter more for women. Correcting for this bias is done in two stages. First, one estimates the probability that the woman will join the wage labor force. Then one estimates the economic returns to her education once she does join by approximating the percentage wage increases associated with it. To separate the two stages of the analysis, one must identify some influence on the decision to participate (such as access to land) that does not also affect wages to distinguish the two stages of the procedure.

2.07 One can see the difference between deflating by labor force participation rates or correcting for the selection bias by estimating the returns for the <u>same</u> countries (in Asia and Latin America) in different ways (see figure 2.1). The returns to male or female schooling change, and the differential may as well. Often the selection-corrected returns to schooling for women exceed those for men, especially at the secondary level. In Thailand, correcting for selection bias tends to reduce the returns for men and women, but the corrected returns above the primary level are much higher for women than for men. The corrected return for secondary education is about 25 percent for women and 7 percent for men; at higher levels of education it is about 18 percent for women and 8 percent for men (Schultz 1989a). In Peru, the returns to female education increase nationwide when corrected for the selection bias, and corrected returns are higher for women than for men at both secondary and higher levels (Khandker 1990). They are surprisingly low for both genders at the primary level.

2.08 The returns to female schooling may also be suppressed by market imperfections that limit women's options more than men's and so reduce women's earnings. Female participation in the wage labor force reflects the difference between the wages women could command in the labor market and the value of their time outside the labor market. Women join the wage labor force if the <u>actual</u> wage rate at least matches the reservation wage (the wage cutoff below which women opt out of the labor market). In fact, the actual wage even for educated women is often below their reservation wage, whereas for men it is usually higher than their reservation wage.

Figure 2.1: Sensitivity of Rates of Return to Alternative Methodologies, Evidence in Asia and Latin America

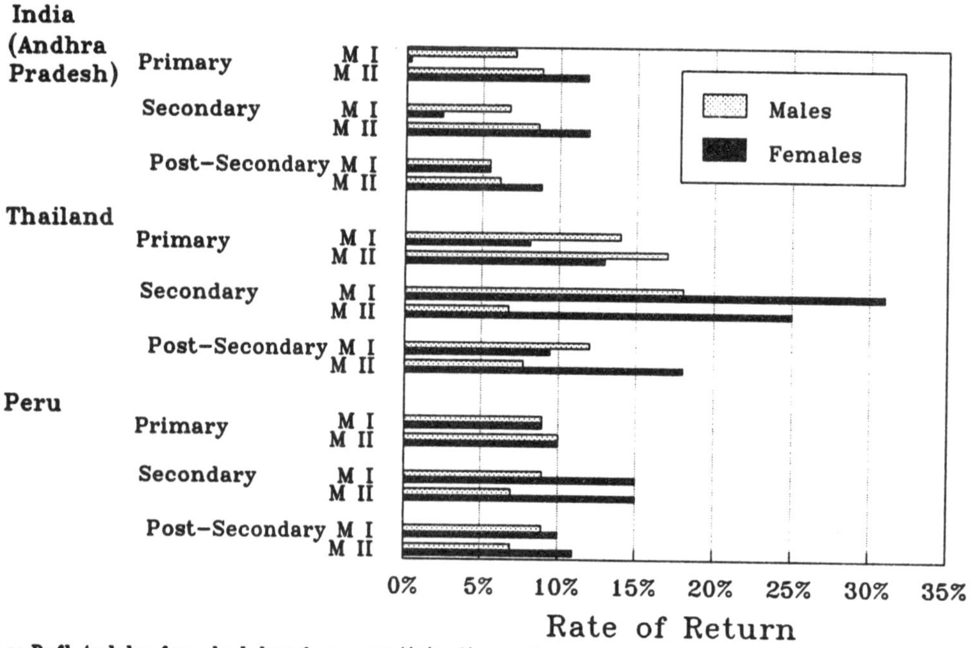

__MI__ = Deflated by female labor force participation rates.
__MII__= Not deflated by female labor force participation rates (and studies in Thailand and Peru correct for selection bias).

__Sources__: Khandker 1990; Schultz 1989a; Tilak 1987.

2.09 Ideally, differences in wage rates should reflect only differences in productivity, determined mainly by people's varying physical and human capital. Most research to explain differences in wage rates between men and women (or among people in general) has therefore focused on productivity. But education and years of experience account for only part of the difference. Substantial unexplained differences in male and female wages remain in many countries and regions. For example, Tilak (1987) demonstrated that the mean earnings for women in India were up to six times lower than those for men with the same level of education and productivity. Sambamoorthi (1984) showed that "discrimination" or other unexplained influences accounted for 21 percent of the male-female wage differential in another region in India. Several recent studies on Latin America, where female enrollment rates are high and gender parity has largely been achieved at the secondary level, show that men out-earn women in similar jobs. Productivity indicators including education and experience explain on average only about one third of the differences in male and female wage rates (Psacharopoulos and Tzannatos, forthcoming).

2.10 Differences in wages for people of comparable education and years of experience may also reflect other influences on productivity, such as interruptions of work or other costs. If women have greater need for health care or maternity leave, for example, these are real costs to employers.

2.11 The differences in wages may also reflect "discrimination" -- labor market restrictions or other market imperfections that limit women's employment prospects in the formal wage labor force, often with a protective intent (see box 2.1). In Bolivia, for instance, men are allowed to work 48 hours a week and women only 40, and most firms are not allowed to have a workforce that is more than 45 percent female. Such restrictions -- even if meant to be beneficial -- can lock women into low-skill, repetitive work that can depress women's productivity and dampen their earning prospects, which may pose a greater threat to women's wellbeing than some forbidden lines of work would (Dixon-Mueller and Anker 1988; ILO 1989).

Box 2.1 "Protective" Legislation and Equal Employment Opportunity for Women

Most countries try to protect women's health by restricting their employment, but the effect may be to unduly limit women's work choices. There is no consensus on the tradeoff between protection and equal opportunity.

The ILO Maximum Weight Convention, 1967 (No.127), and its accompanying Recommendation (No. 128) state that women should carry loads no heavier than 55 kilograms, less than the maximum for men, and many national laws reflect this convention. In 1987, 91 countries prohibited underground work for women of any age for reasons considered to relate to morals, economics, and health. Some 100 countries prohibit women's employment in work other than underground or manual load-handling which is considered dangerous, arduous, unhealthy, or unpleasant; but these prohibitions often do not appear to be based on scientific or medical justifications. Some 20 countries forbid employing women in processes involving machinery, 8 exclude women from loading or unloading ships, and 13 restrict women using wheeled transport. Several countries prohibit women from employment in fields considered to pose a "moral danger." These vary by country but include sale of alcoholic beverages or work in outdoor shops at night.

For understandable reasons, many countries also have laws and regulations aimed to restrict employment to protect pregnant women or nursing mothers. Some also exclude women of childbearing age from certain lines of work or contact with chemicals. These laws have varying degrees of scientific justification. Other laws require maternity leave, benefits, restrooms, and the like.

More recently, a number of countries have determined that "protective" laws are excessively restrictive of women's work options and have moved to reconsider some, especially those not directly concerned with pregnancy and maternity.

Source: ILO 1989.

2.12 When women face barriers to joining the wage labor force, education may raise women's productivity more outside the wage labor force than in it. Women may then opt out of the wage labor force. Estimates of the returns to female schooling based on such imperfect labor markets will probably be lower than in markets where women face fewer barriers.

2.13 Women also face barriers to productive self-employment that constrain their earnings as farmers or entrepreneurs and so limit the returns to female education. A full discussion of these issues is beyond the scope of this paper, but a few points should be kept in mind. For instance, research shows that women farmers often have less access than men farmers do to information, technology, inputs, land, and markets (see, for example, World Bank Kenya: The Role of Women in Development 1989; World Bank Women in Pakistan 1989; World Bank Gender and Poverty in India, 1991).[2]

---

[2] For instance, an ILO study of Botswana in 1974-75 reports the value of livestock, land, and equipment of households headed by women (28 percent of the total) was about one-third to one-half that of households headed by men on a per-household, per-person, and per-adult basis (Dixon-Mueller and Anker 1988; ILO, 1989). In Kenya, a study from the 1970's shows two-thirds of women who head households had farms of less than one hectare, compared to 45 percent of men; 90 percent of the female heads of household had no education compared to 55 percent of men (Barnes and Warner 1982). Another study of Kenya shows farms headed by women (40 percent of the total in the area studied) used significantly less inputs and had less land per person; but when women and men farmers had similar access to land, input, education, and the like, women outproduced men by 6 percent (in yields per acre) (Moock 1973).

Extension programs are sometimes designed deliberately to reach men, on the dubious theory that the men will pass along information to their wives. This is no help to women who head households and is demonstrably ineffective for wives as well (Baxter 1986; Saito and Weidemann 1990; Saito and Spurling, 1991). Even when extension programs try to reach women as well as men, they may not cover crops or tasks of particular interest to women, and they may not consider cultural constraints that affect how women farmers may deal with male extension agents. Many women farmers or entrepreneurs also have more difficulty than men in gaining access to formal credit, for several reasons. Women lack the legal title to assets needed as collateral for loans (Saito and Spurling, 1991; Holt and Ribe 1991). The practical problems of traveling with children to formal credit institutions, women's lack of education, and traditional attitudes also impede women's access to formal credit. This lack of access to information, resources, and markets effectively restricts many women to low-productivity, low-paying lines of work. When women are unable to produce or earn much despite long hours spent working, the returns to female schooling are further depressed. Estimating the returns to education in self-employment may require valuing nonmarketed output -- often an impossible task, given scarce data and the difficulty of using prices as proxies. The few studies that focus on self-employed men and women suggest that education pays off for women, sometimes more and sometimes less than for men (Moock 1973; Herz and Khandker 1991; Khandker 1990).

2.14 Macroeconomic policy distortions may exacerbate the differences in male and female productivity, and hence in returns to schooling. For example, if most women work in fields such as agriculture that are penalized by taxation or pricing policies, while most men (especially educated men) work in protected sectors (such as industry or the public sector), then returns to women's education may be more depressed than returns to men's. In a study of Kenya in the 1960s when agriculture was heavily disprotected and a high proportion of women were farmers, the returns on primary and secondary schooling for women were 7.1 percent and 19.5 percent, respectively; the numbers for men were 21.7 percent and 23.6 percent. But in countries with macroeconomic policies more favorable to agriculture, which women dominated -- for example, in Taiwan, Thailand and South Korea -- women's rates of return exceeded men's (Schultz 1989a). In India, men dominate the heavily protected manufacturing industry and public sector employment and most women work in the unorganized agricultural and informal sectors. Not surprisingly, Indian women's earnings and hence their returns to schooling are compressed.

2.15 The economic policy imperfections, labor-market barriers, limited access to information and resources, and shortfalls in education may combine to lock women into low-productivity work as farmers, small-scale entrepreneurs, or casual laborers. A recent study on Bombay, India, demonstrates such a pattern (Khandker 1991). In many African and Asian countries, most women are self-employed or casual laborers.

2.16 A vicious cycle may result: men earn more, making the returns to male schooling higher, so boys are sent to school more often than girls. Girls then grow up lacking the education they need to compete. Cultural traditions may reflect and reinforce economics, especially in poor rural settings (see box 2.2).

Box 2.2 Returns to Schooling, Employment Prospects, and Social Attitudes

Two studies from India show that a woman's labor supply rises with increases in the wage rate she can command, which reflects her education. As women's earnings rise, their fertility tends to fall (Khandker forthcoming; Malathy 1989). Another study finds that secondary and university education encourages urban women to participate in the labor force in Pakistan (Kozel and Alderman 1988).

In rural Pakistan, however, the constraints are more severe. Few women work for wages; most work in home-based productive activities and spend 25-30 hours weekly in chores. A woman's monthly household labor declines 1.1 days for each girl aged 10-15 in the family, but a teen-age boy adds as much work as a child 5-9 years old. A child's illness adds .5 days labor for each woman in the household, but the woman's own illness does not affect her labor. The provision of electricity increases the time women spend working, because she can work more after dark. In these circumstances, education hardly affects the likelihood of the woman joining the wage labor force, though it leads to more days worked if she does join. She works one day less in the household for every day of labor force activities.

As the rural Pakistani woman's education increases, given the current social conditions, the main effect is to increase her leisure or her "management activities" at home. Education raises her reservation wage for participating in the labor force and may even reinforce traditions that discourage female labor force participation or traditional chores. As the researchers note:

> This gets to the policy crux. Most rural jobs in Pakistan for which education is an obvious advantage, and which are compatible with the social roles of women and their reluctance to travel outside the village, are government jobs with requirements for higher levels of education than observed here, such as teaching and health professions. The investment -- and risk -- that is necessary for women to obtain sufficient education to participate in this portion of the labor market may be prohibitive for most families if, in fact, the possibility is even locally feasible.
>
> There may be a circular trap to overcome. Few women obtain an education because the private returns are insufficient. The private returns are insufficient, in part, because education rates are sufficiently low that the village setting has not responded with a socially regarded role for educated women outside of a few possibilities.
>
> This situation may be changing as female school participation rates are rising, although rural women with a secondary school education are still a rarity. The government may have a role in promoting this change. Not only will increased investment in schooling lower the private costs, but it may be worthwhile to consider the implication of lowering the requirements for employment in the type of rural-based jobs the government provides. This ... must be carefully evaluated. Moreover, some demonstration effects of local women being employed within their own community may encourage women to seek other employment opportunities.... Until women see education in their private interest -- either in terms of social advantage or financial advantage -- schooling may be constrained by demand as much as supply considerations (Alderman and Chisti 1989, 19-21).

Sources: Alderman and Chisti 1989; Khandker 1991; Kozel and Alderman 1988; Malathy 1989.

2.17 It is not easy to break this cycle. But part of the answer is to cease protecting certain sectors, remove the labor market barriers, and try to promote women's access to education, information, and resources so that they gain mobility and can escape the low-productivity, low-paying sectors. Then the returns to female education ought to rise and generate greater demand for schooling. In Malaysia, for example, the government promoted education and employment opportunities for both men and women in the 1970s, and economic growth was relatively rapid. The largest contributions to household income growth were from women wage earners -- from 4.3 percent in 1973 to 12.9 percent in 1987. Women shifted from self-employment and casual labor into the formal wage sector, and the private returns to education increased for females and slightly increased for males between 1973 and 1987 (World Bank 1991a). More research is needed to show a) how macroeconomic policies and better access to information and resources affect women's earnings (absolutely and compared to men) and b) how that affects the private returns to male and female schooling. But economic logic suggests that promoting schooling for both men and women will produce a more efficient economy.

Social Returns to Female Education

2.18 The social rate of return to education is defined as the internal rate of return that equates the total costs to society with the total benefits. Governments typically incur heavy costs for education. These costs must be included along with the costs to families in estimating social returns. If benefits were left unchanged, this increase in costs would reduce the social returns below the level of the private returns. These may be called "partial social returns" (see table 2.2). They will be similar for men and women only if the costs to governments of educating boys and girls are the same. But increasing girls' education may require special steps that incur at least modest additional costs, as discussed below.

Table 2.2: Partial Social and Private Rates of Returns to Education by School Level mean number (number of countries reported in parentheses)

	Social			Private		
Region	Primary	Secondary	Higher	Primary	Secondary	Higher
Africa	27	19	14	45	28	33
	(12)	(12)	(12)	(9)	(9)	(9)
Asia	18	14	12	34	15	18
	(9)	(11)	(11)	(5)	(8)	(8)
Latin America	35	19	16	61	28	26
	(8)	(8)	(8)	(5)	(5)	(5)
High-income	13[b]	10	8	19[b]	12	11
countries[a]	(6)	(15)	(15)	(7)	(14)	(15)

[a]Europe, United States, New Zealand, Israel.
[b]Not calculable in most high-income countries where the comparison group without a primary education is small and highly unrepresentative at younger ages.

Source: Schultz 1989a.

2.19 To estimate the full social returns, the benefits should also be adjusted to use wages net of taxes. Often this refinement is ignored, and gross wage rates are used. But if the private returns are net of taxes, then the social returns should add any net increases in tax revenues resulting from better jobs or higher earnings that education made possible. This adjustment is also rarely done. To the extent that more women than men stay out of the labor force because of poor education, increasing female participation in the labor force through education should increase the net taxes from women more than men, so that this adjustment will raise the returns to female schooling relative to those from male schooling.

2.20 More fundamentally, to estimate full social returns, the benefits should also include the social benefits or externalities arising from education, such as better health and lower fertility. These social benefits are generally greater for female education than for male education. But social benefits are hard to value in economic terms, and estimates of social returns are rarely attempted. As a result, the "social returns" are sometimes said -- mistakenly -- to fall short of the private returns, and policy makers pay too little attention to true social gains.

2.21 To get an idea of the magnitude of the social benefits of girls' schooling, research on its impact on health and fertility should be understood even if it cannot be valued in economic terms. A considerable body of such research exists.

Maternal Education and Child Health

2.22 Research for different countries suggests that on average, an additional year's schooling for women is associated with a 5 to 10 percent reduction in child mortality under 5 years of age (Cochrane 1979; Schultz 1989a). Two major cross-country studies (Cochrane, O'Hara, and Leslie 1980, 1982) conclude that maternal education is a robust determinant of child health and that the effect of men's education on child health appears to be much weaker. This is not surprising, given that the primary health worker for most children is their mother. Another major study (Mensch, Lentzner, and Presto 1986) examined the socioeconomic differentials in child mortality in 15 developing countries. Based on time series, this study was methodologically more advanced. It also reported maternal education's significant impact on child survival. Studies of individual countries confirm the role of maternal education.

2.23 Some studies may exaggerate the role of maternal education because they omit other explanatory variables that education may mask. If these missing variables really account for much of the apparent impact of maternal education, then increasing education may not have the hoped-for effect on children's health. Unfortunately, it is hard to identify what those other variables may be, much less to measure them. Thus both conceptual and empirical problems make it difficult to isolate the impact of education. Some research tries to net out other variables without identifying them by using "fixed-effects" models, thereby taking a much more conservative view of the role of female education, but this research has its own methodological dilemmas. For instance, some fixed-effects approaches require that samples be severely restricted, which may distort their findings (Behrman 1991). One study on Brazil avoids this dilemma by assuming that parental height can represent other family characteristics that could influence children's schooling. It concludes that maternal education has a strong influence on children's survival, especially in poorer areas (Thomas and others 1990).

2.24 A recent study in India tried to isolate the effects of mothers' schooling on infant mortality at the regional level (Beenstock and Sturdy 1990). Adult female literacy, DPT vaccination, poverty, caste and the use of medical facilities emerged as important determinants of infant mortality. Two basic findings remained unaffected despite the inclusion of many other "controlling variables": the illiteracy of mothers contributed to higher levels of infant mortality; and the risk of infants dying was significantly higher when mothers married before the age of 18. Given that girls' education leads to a later marriage age, female education could substantially help lower infant mortality.

2.25 The growing research on how maternal education works to improve children's health also reinforces the view that maternal education matters. Mothers' education may affect children's health and learning by at least four routes. It may increase the economic resources available to the household. It may supplement the productivity of already available health inputs by improving mothers' nonmarket productivity. Given prices and income, it may influence household spending (preferences) in favor of goods consumed by children (as opposed to adult goods). Finally, it may also enhance households' willingness to make human capital investments in children, especially girls.

2.26 Recent research on Africa concludes that educated mothers are more likely to seek health care for their children once the children are sick (Collier 1991a,b). A number of recent studies suggest that income under the control of the mother is more likely to affect children's health. For example, a recent study using Brazilian data (Thomas and others 1990) indicates that women's unearned income has a much larger effect on children's survival than men's. The effects of maternal income on both sons and daughters exceeds the effects of paternal income. This is because mothers spend four to seven times proportionately more on food from incremental incomes compared with fathers. Moreover, mothers' unearned income has a greater impact on daughters than sons, and fathers' unearned income has a greater impact on sons (Thomas and others 1990 -- see box 2.3). A study from India shows that as the proportion of women in the wage labor force increases, the survival rates for girls begins to catch up with that of boys (Rosenzweig and Schultz 1982).

2.27 But modeling how maternal education may improve children's health is conceptually and empirically formidable. So most researchers resort to some type of "reduced form" -- that is, they investigate the impact of female education without fully modeling the process. These studies confirm that maternal education positively affects children's health and nutritional outcomes, but differ on the exact magnitudes of the effects and the importance of other influences.

Box 2.3 Like Mother, Like Daughter?

A recent study using household survey data from Brazil, Ghana, and the United States suggests that mothers devote more resources to the health of their daughters and fathers prefer to allocate resources to their sons. The study finds that the education of the mother in all three countries has a bigger effect on her daughter's health and nutritional status as proxied by height; her education has much less effect on her son's height. The fathers's education, by contrast, has far more effect on his son's height than on his daughter's. The only exception found is in rural Brazil, where the father's education does not affect sons' or daughters' height, but the mother's education affects both, especially sons'. Households apparently allocate resources differently depending on the gender of the child and the parent. In Ghana, the education of a woman who has more schooling than her husband influences a daughter's height more than a son's height. In Brazil, women's non-labor income has a positive effect on the health of her daughter but not on her son's health. If relative education and the non-labor income of spouses indicate power or influence in "household bargaining," this research suggests that gender differences in resource allocations affect both the efficiency of child care and differences in parental preferences. No such research has been done for South Asia, where the mortality rates of girls are abnormally high compared to those for boys.

Source: Thomas 1990.

Maternal Education and Children's Learning

2.28 Several studies summarized by Behrman (1991) suggest that parental schooling promotes children's schooling: Birdsall (1980) on Colombia; Wolfe and Behrman (1984) on Nicaragua; Birdsall (1980, 1985) on Brazil; King and Lillard (1983, 1987) on Malaysia and the Philippines; Behrman and Sussangkarn (1989) on Thailand; and King and Bellew on Peru (1990).

2.29 The 1980 study of Brazil finds an additional year of parental schooling linked to an additional .04 to .11 years of child schooling in urban areas and .14 to .39 years of child schooling in rural areas. The impact of maternal education is significantly larger than father's schooling (controlling for paternal income, mother's age, child's age and sex, and recent migration). Controlling for the quality of schooling strengthens the effect of maternal education in urban areas (Birdsall 1980).

2.30 Research from Thailand shows that, controlling for household income and age, the schooling continuation rate rises 0.023 for every year of the father's schooling and 0.0193 for every year of the mother's schooling. The mother's and father's education are closer substitutes when the quality of education is similar (Behrman and Sussangkarn 1989).

2.31 Among Malay and Chinese children in Malaysia, the mother's schooling significantly affects the daughter's schooling. Among Chinese and Filipino children, the mother's and father's schooling both matter, suggesting differences in the three cultures (King and Lillard 1987).

2.32 The study of the effects of maternal schooling on Peruvian children's schooling looks at different age-cohorts. It finds generally significant effects for both maternal and paternal schooling, which decline substantially across age-cohorts. For instance, the impact on females (males) of an additional year of maternal schooling is 0.33 years (0.29) for the 1925-39 cohort, and 0.12 (0.18) for the 1960-66. Maternal education matters more for daughters and paternal education more for sons, but the father's presence in the family matters for daughters (King and Bellew 1990). The study suggests these results show that the expansion of public schooling in Peru combined with better quality of schooling (see box 4.2 in chapter 4) reduced the importance of parental education.

2.33 A new study of Ghana finds that maternal education is the main influence on children's schooling, whether for boys or girls. But the effect on girls is roughly twice as great -- whether for girls' actual enrollment or for the probability that the girls will continue to the next grade. Paternal education also promotes children's enrollment, more for girls than for boys, but the maternal effects are stronger (Lavy forthcoming).

Female Education and Family Size

2.34 Research shows convincingly that women's education leads to smaller families, while men's education has less effect (World Bank 1980d, 1986d; Schultz 1989a). The logic is straightforward. Parenting requires more time from women. They bear the children and breastfeed and while the division of labor among parents for the care of older children varies across cultures, it is mainly women who care for young children. Education increases the opportunity cost of the mother's time. It opens up new opportunities for her to gain income or standing, and those compete with childbearing and child care. Education encourages her to delay marriage to begin with and to have fewer children once married. By contrast, new opportunities for men to earn more do not compete as much with their parenting role, since they spent less time with the children to begin with. Indeed, men may want more children as their income or wealth rises.

2.35 The fertility-reducing effects of female education should be stronger where women can rely more on contraceptives and less on long-term breastfeeding to achieve their desired family size. If education encourages women to enter the labor force, and if they tend to breastfeed less, fertility (and abortion) rates could rise if women lack regular access to safe and effective contraception.

2.36 Research reported in two World Development Reports (World Bank 1980d, 1984f) and a policy paper on population for Africa (World Bank 1986a) confirms that female education reduces fertility, especially where family planning services are available. Female education is linked with later marriage, lower fertility rates, the desire for smaller families, increased practice of contraception, and generally increased practice of more effective methods of contraception. The relationship is stronger as women's education increases.

2.37 In some countries, however, where few women are educated and poverty is widespread, a small increase in female education may be linked to an increase in fertility. This phenomenon disappears as education levels rise and as research takes better account of the husband's income and education (Schultz 1989a). As with education and child mortality, it is possible that education masks other underlying influences on fertility. But studies netting out other possible influences on fertility that education might mask still conclude that the fertility impact of female education is robust (Behrman 1990; Schultz 1989a).

2.38 Part of the fertility effects from education come from women's increased earning capability; fertility tends to fall as women's wages (rise but rises as husband's wages increase or as the family's landholdings increase) (Schultz 1989a; World Bank 1980d, 1984f; Duraiswamy 1989).

2.39 Until recently, some research suggested that in Africa, education was not so strongly associated with fertility declines. Total fertility rates and desired family size were high on average for women at all educational levels. But in the past few years as female education has increased, family planning services have been improved and expanded, and the patterns in Africa have begun to resemble the patterns elsewhere. In Kenya, for example, where progress in education and in family planning services has been relatively rapid, more educated women want and have smaller families and use more contraception. The national fertility rate has dropped precipitously (World Bank Kenya: The Role of Women in Economic Development 1989; Demographic and Health Surveys 1990a,b). One recent study (Schultz 1989a) has assembled the available data for some countries in Africa, Latin America, and the Caribbean (figure 2.2).

Figure 2.2: Women's Education Affects Total and Desired Fertility

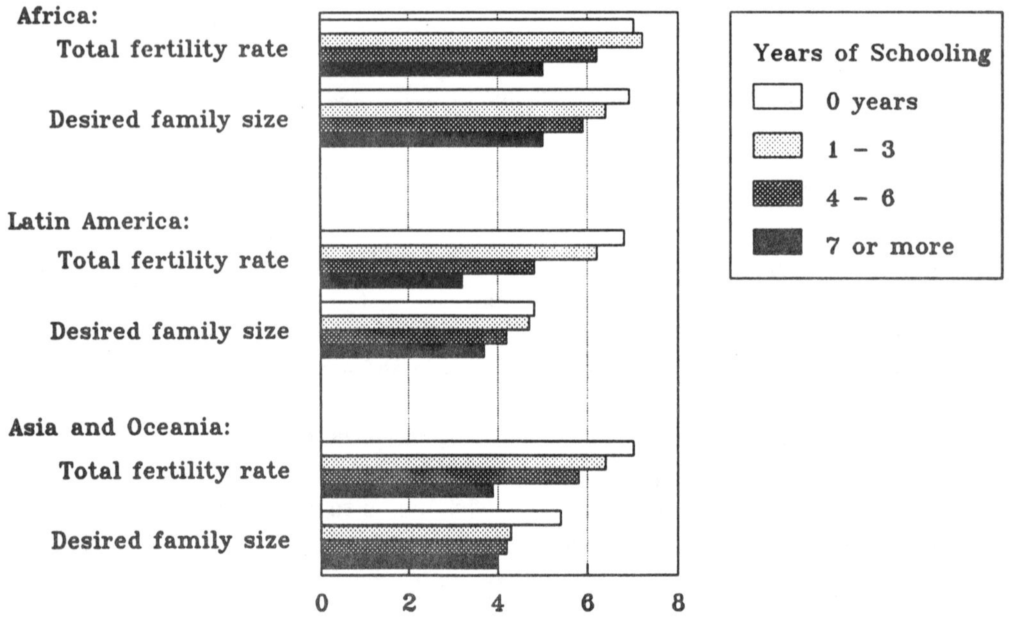

Source: Schultz 1989a.

2.40 The average level of education in a community may affect individual attitudes toward family size and family planning through some "threshold effects." In other words, women with X years of education may have different numbers of children depending on how much education other women also have and what this has done to general attitudes toward childbearing. Figure 2.3 shows that within each region (including Africa) countries with a higher proportion of educated women have lower total fertility rates and higher contraceptive prevalence rates. While this is encouraging, more detailed research is needed to show whether community threshold effects play a role in reducing fertility.

Figure 2.3: Fertility & Family Planning in Countries Ranked* by Women's Education

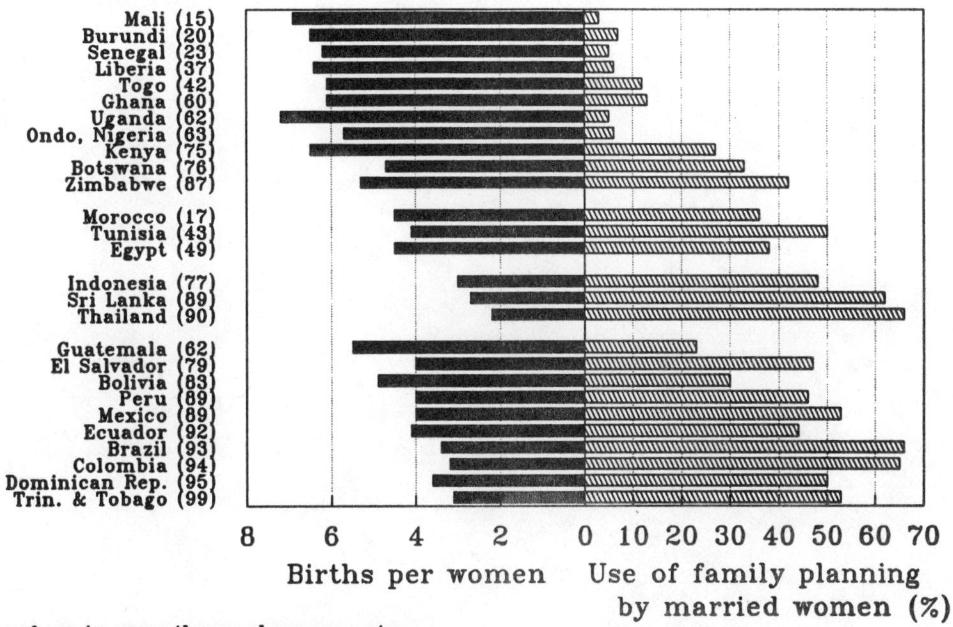

* Numbers in parentheses show percentage of women (15–49) with some education.

Source: Demographic & Health Surveys 1990a,b.

2.41 In-depth country studies reinforce the point that women with more education have fewer children. In almost every country studied in recent years, educated women have fewer children than uneducated women. In Brazil, for example, uneducated women have on average 6.5 children; those with a secondary education have on average 2.5. In Liberia, women who have been to secondary school are ten times more likely to use family planning than women have not been to school at all. Evidence across Indian states suggests that literate women have considerably lower age-specific fertility rates than illiterate women, controlling for age. In Kenya and Indonesia, evidence also shows that educated women not only want smaller families but are more willing to use modern effective means of contraception. These studies suggest that secondary education often has a much greater influence on family size than primary schooling.

The Female Education Paradox

2.42 In sum, the returns to female schooling (especially secondary) are plain. Private economic returns are similar for men and women, and often higher in countries where most educational resources now go to boys. The social returns to female education are high and exceed those to male education: female education improves children's health, reduces the number of unwanted births and causes women to want smaller families. The potential for more productive labor, better health, and slower population growth all argue for more investment in female education. Why then do governments and families still provide less schooling for girls than for boys in much of the developing world? The principal explanations are explored in the next chapter.

CHAPTER 3. CONSTRAINTS ON FEMALE EDUCATION

3.01 What constrains investments in female schooling? The answer lies in a deeper understanding of the apparent returns -- who gains from education in what ways, and who bears the costs, both economic and social.

3.02 In assessing the private return on an investment, one normally assumes that the investor who covers the costs reaps the gains. Most estimates of the private returns to schooling assume that the only private cost of schooling is income foregone by the student. But this is inaccurate. The family actually pays for much of the cost of education, and immediately. Yet the gains accrue mainly to the student, as an adult, and to his or her children -- the grandchildren of the parents who paid for the schooling. From the families' perspective, the costs of educating girls are likely to be higher and the benefits more tenuous than for boys. In short, the private economic return from educating daughters may be less than that from educating sons. This discrepancy is greater and matters more in poor families. From the families' perspective, if not from society's, education for girls may seem a less attractive investment than education for boys. And where education is not effectively compulsory, it is the family -- especially the parents -- who usually decide how much education their children will receive.

The Parental Decision: A Balancing Test

3.03 In deciding whether to send a child to school, parents weigh the advantages of keeping the child at home against the advantages of whatever schooling is available. Changes in either side of the balance can tip decisions for or against schooling.

3.04 The advantages of keeping a child home include the work the child can do, the income the child can earn, and the income the parents can earn because the child does tasks the parents would otherwise have to do. Also, school fees and other direct costs of schooling can be avoided. The advantages to parents of sending a child to school include the satisfaction they feel in seeing the child prosper and possibly such tangible benefits as remittances from children's earnings as the parents age.

3.05 Constraints to schooling (see table 3.1) thus include:

- The direct costs to parents of schooling such as fees, books, and clothing.
- The opportunity costs of children's time in school -- which in most poor families are likely to be higher for girls.
- The costs of observing cultural traditions and ensuring children's safety (also likely to be higher for girls).
- The limited economic opportunities that especially affect girls' earning potential and thus returns on their schooling.

Table 3.1 Constraints on Girls' School Attendance

TYPICAL CONSTRAINTS INFLUENCING PARENTAL DECISIONS:

Direct Costs	Opportunity Costs	Limited Economic Returns
For example, for fees, books, clothing, and to address cultural and safety concerns.	Chore time, sibling care, foregone earnings (girls' and mothers').	Macroeconomic policies, limited access to labor markets and resources, quality of education

Costs of Schooling

3.06 The family bears several kinds of costs for their children's schooling. Economic evidence suggests that parents weigh these costs against potential benefits; their income-elasticity of demand is often higher for girls' schooling than for boys (see, for example, DeTray 1988 on Malaysia). The costs to parents of educating their children include direct and indirect (opportunity) costs.

Direct Costs of Schooling

3.07 The direct costs of schooling include school fees, books, paper, pencils, tutoring, and required clothing. The lower the family's income, the more difficult it is to cover these costs. Actual expenditures on schooling amount to about 4 percent of household consumption in low-income countries, 6 percent in middle-income countries, and 8 percent in industrial countries (World Bank 1990n). There is wide variance around the mean. In India and Pakistan, for instance, with per capita GNP of about $350, education accounts for 3-4 percent of household consumption compared with 9 percent in Kenya ($370) and 13 percent in Zambia ($290). Among countries with per capita GNP of $1,200-1,300, education accounts for 9 percent of household consumption in Tunisia, 1 percent in Turkey, and 6 percent in Peru. The direct costs are generally similar for boys and girls.

Opportunity Costs of Schooling

3.08 Because poor families rely more on each family member to contribute to the family's survival, the opportunity costs of educating children are higher for poor families. They are also higher for girls. The opportunity costs include lost chore time, children's foregone earnings, and -- especially for girls -- mothers' foregone earnings.

3.09 Throughout most of Sub-Saharan Africa and South Asia, the heavy work burden of rural women may force them to keep their daughters at home to help with care of younger siblings, time-consuming tasks on the farm, and such household chores as cleaning, cooking, and collecting fuel. Research from Malawi shows that school-age girls spend more time than boys on household chores, and spend less time the first hour after school on studying or relaxing (Davison and Kanyuka 1990 in Grant-Lewis 1990). In Burkina Faso, time-use studies reveal that girls from the age of 7 on spend 3.5 hours a day on household tasks compared with only 1.5 hours for boys (Sajogyo and others 1980 in FAO 1985). In the Gambia, 10 percent of female dropouts from primary school are said to drop out to stay home to care for siblings (World Bank 1990i).

3.10 In Nepal, studies have documented that the demand for girls' labor exceeds the demand for boys' labor by half (Jamison and Lockheed 1987). In India, Bangladesh, and Nepal, by the age of 5 many girls are involved in such household responsibilities as collecting water and fuel and managing younger siblings and farm activities. Between the ages of 10 and 15, girls may work 8 to 10 hours a day on productive activities inside and outside the home (Cain 1977; Rosenweig 1980; Acharya and Bennett 1981). Time-use studies in India have shown that younger girls worked 5.5 hours and older girls 7.7 hours a day in adult household and agricultural tasks, whereas younger boys spent only 1.8 hours and older boys 3.6 hours on such tasks (World Bank Gender and Poverty in India 1991).

3.11 In general, girls do more chores than boys. Girls care for siblings, fetch wood and water, and in other ways that ease their mother's drudgery. They also contribute to household production by caring for animals, pounding grain, and so forth. Time allocation studies have shown that in settings as different as Nepal and Kenya, girls get involved in household production tasks at a much younger age and work longer hours than boys. Many girls are classified as "nonworking" (not in the wage labor force), but most girls from poor families spend substantial amounts of time running the household. In rural Java (Indonesia), girls aged 10 to 15 in the poorest households worked an average of 94 hours a month, compared with 70 hours in middle-income households and 26 hours in the wealthiest households. The corresponding averages for boys' household labor were 38 hours, 8 hours, and 9 hours, respectively (Sajogyo and others 1980 in FAO 1985).

3.12 In some regions, boys and girls specialize in their contributions to the family, and boys work more in the wage labor force. In the Philippines, among children aged 12 to 14, girls spend more than twice the hours in household activities than boys do, but girls work half as much in the labor force (Evenson and others 1980). In Bangladesh girls 13 to 15 spend ten times as many hours as boys in household activities, but boys spend twice as much time in crop production and about five times as much time in wage work (Pitt and Rozenzweig 1989). But poor families in Asia also receive some cash income from girls. Extreme household poverty often forces girls to enter the labor markets at a young age. In India, 1981 data show that of the girls aged 11 to 13, 24.3 percent of those in rural areas and 9.3 percent in urban areas were in the wage labor force (World Bank Gender and Poverty in India 1991). In Latin America, the roles seem sometimes to be reversed. Among Peruvian children out of school, 30 percent of girls aged 5 to 7 and 50 percent of girls 8 to 10 reported working for wages, slightly higher percentages than reported for boys (see box 3.1 -- King and Bellew 1991 in Herz and Khandker 1991).

Box 3.1 School-Age Girls in Peru's Labor Market

Among children aged 11-13 in Peru, only 26 percent of girls reported no time in the labor market, compared with 35 percent of boys. Among children out of school, 15 percent of boys aged 11-13 and 31% of boys aged 14-16 report no time worked at home, compared with 8 percent and 9 percent of girls. Even girls in school were working: 11 percent of girls 5 to 7, 25 percent of girls 8 to 10, and 34 percent of girls 11 to 13. But the percentages are higher for boys attending school: 19 percent (ages 5 to 7), 28 percent (8 to 10), and 48 percent (11 to 13). In addition to market work, girls older than 8 work more hours at home. Some 28 percent of boys aged 8 to 10 who attend school report no hours worked at home, compared to 18% for girls. Finally, 19 percent of boys aged 11 to 13 and 21 percent of those aged 14 to 16 report no time worked at home, compared with 9 percent and 8 percent for girls.

Source: King and Bellew 1991 in Herz and Khandker 1991.

3.13 Girls' household activities, especially in Asia and Africa, seem to have more impact than boys' activities on the parents' earnings (Hyde 1989). Girls' work at home often permits parents, especially mothers, to work more on the farm or in the labor force. In sending girls to school, the family loses the income that the mother might have earned because the daughter substituted for the mother in doing home chores. This is particularly true among poor families, where girls' labor may be crucial to family survival. Micro-level research in India has shown that girls can handle women's work in agricultural operations: a 10 percent increase in female wages lowers the school attendance rate of girls from poor families by about 5 percent (Rosenzweig 1980). A study from Botswana shows that the enrollment of children is sensitive to the presence of grandparents or other elders who eliminate or reduce the need for child labor (Chernikovsky 1985). Girls are also withdrawn from the labor force or school more often than boys to substitute for their mothers in caring for younger siblings who fall ill (see box 3.2). In principle the picture might be similar for sons and is -- for example, in Ethiopia and Botswana, where boys or men traditionally herd cattle (Chernikovsky 1985). But in practice the picture for sons in many countries is different from that for girls. Sons do fewer chores at home and so do not liberate either parent to earn more. The full opportunity cost of educating girls may thus be higher than that for boys, especially for poor families. This difference may help explain why poor parents often invest less in their daughter's schooling than in their son's.

Box 3.2 Older Sisters' Care of Young Siblings

A recent study from Indonesia shows that families rely much more on older sisters than on older brothers to care for young siblings. Fewer than 3 percent of male siblings aged 14-18 are involved in household care, compared with 25 percent of the girls. Half the girls attend school compared with 61 percent of the boys, and 29 percent of the boys are in the labor force compared with 16 percent of girls. Twenty-four percent of mothers are in the labor force and 75 percent are in household care. When infants fall ill, teenage brothers do not stop their education or work to help out. The probability of the mother being in the labor force drops 63 percent (from 24 percent to 15 percent) when the incidence of childhood illness rises 29 percent (one standard deviation). The probability of a daughter aged 14-18 being in the labor force drops 25 percent (from 16 percent to 12 percent) and the probability of her attending school drops by 15 percent. Her probability of participating in home care rises by 53 percent. As teenage children age, boys leave school and enter the labor market, but girls leave school, reduce their leisure, and participate more in household activities. If daughters can stay home to care for young siblings, mothers can spend more time at work. Other research on the Philippines notes that families spent 23 percent less time caring for young girls than for young boys.

Sources: Evenson and others 1980; Pitt and Rosenzweig 1989.

3.14 Most analysts do not recognize differences in the opportunity costs of educating boys and girls. Because data on children's wages are scarce, they value the time any child spends at school by using wage rates for uneducated adults. If families rely on girls to substitute for mothers' household tasks and this allows mothers to work, it is appropriate to value a girl's time at school at a woman's wage. But if boys do not substitute for fathers similarly, then it is not appropriate to value a boy's time at a man's wage. Doing so overestimates the opportunity cost of educating boys. Instead, boys' actual wages should be used -- and because far more boys than girls do earn wages, boys' wages are often observable. Thus, the opportunity cost of educating boys is likely to be lower than for girls wherever parents rely more on girls to do chores so parents can work. Research is needed that incorporates this difference and assesses the resulting impact on costs and hence returns to schooling.

Traditional Constraints

3.15 Girls have special needs for physical protection, and tradition often demands special concern for girls' privacy and social reputations. In cultures where female seclusion is practiced, the impact of that tradition on girls' enrollment after puberty is likely to be substantial (Kelly and Elliott 1982; El Sanabary 1989; World Bank Bangladesh: Strategies for Enhancing the Role of Women 1990; World Bank Women in Pakistan 1989; World Bank Gender and Poverty in India 1991; Stromquist 1987). Safety and cultural concerns may leave parents feeling obliged not to send girls to school, even when the opportunity cost of girls' chore time is low, unless schools are located close to home, equipped with facilities such as separate lavatories for girls, well supervised, and served by female teachers. When parents themselves lack education, they may be more reluctant to challenge tradition to educate their daughters (Csapo 1981; Callaway 1984 in Hyde 1989). Traditional constraints are likely to be far more severe in rural areas (see box 3.3 on Pakistan).

Distance to Schools

3.16 The closer the school is to home, the less parents tend to worry about girls' safety or reputations because girls can be kept under closer watch. Where transport is difficult or costly and where populations are dispersed, distance is likely to matter more. Empirical evidence exists on the binding nature of this constraint (see, for example, Stromquist 1987). In Egypt, the location of a school within 1 km of a community resulted in an enrollment rate of 94 percent for boys and 74 percent for girls; when the distance was 2 km., boys enrollment fell only slightly to 90 percent, but girls' enrollment plummeted to 64 percent (Robinson and others 1987). In Ghana, a long distance to primary school significantly deters girls' enrollment, but not boys'; and the closer the secondary school, the more likely children are to be sent to primary school, whether they are boys or girls (Lavy forthcoming).

Separate Facilities

3.17 Parents are unlikely to send girls to school if girls lack private lavatories. In some countries, such as Bangladesh, girls must walk to a neighbor or to their own home when they lack lavatories. In others, such as Pakistan, girls are seldom allowed to walk very far.

Box 3.3 Constraints on Female Education in Pakistan

In rural Pakistan only about one-fourth of girls of primary-school age attend schools compared with two-thirds of boys. Only 3 percent of rural girls are still in school by age 12 and fewer than 1 percent by age 14. Fewer than one in six girls complete five years of education, normally considered the minimum for achieving basic literacy.

Such practices as early marriage, lack of opportunity for women in the labor force, and "marrying out" prevent parents from reaping a return on investments in their daughters' educations. Seclusion of women, practiced to varying degrees, hinders female education because it requires female teachers, separate lavatories, and separate schools after puberty if not at the primary level. Yet only a third of rural teachers are female, 90 percent of primary schools lacked lavatories in 1987, and few girls' schools were available.

Moreover, the direct costs of schooling can come to 20 percent of the income of a poor rural family with four children -- and the total fertility rate in Pakistan is 6.8. Finally, girls contribute heavily at home, through household chores and home-based production.

Sources: UNICEF 1987c; World Bank Women in Pakistan 1989.

Female Teachers

3.18 In some settings, girls must be taught by women; in others, parents strongly prefer that girls be taught by women. In Pakistan and Bangladesh, cultural requirements strongly favor female teachers for girls, but only about a third of primary school teachers in Pakistan and a fifth of those in Bangladesh are women (World Bank Bangladesh: Strategies for Enhancing the Role of Women in Development 1990; World Bank Women in Pakistan 1989). In Kenya girls may be taught by men but parents worry about possible pregnancies (World Bank Kenya: The Role of Women in Development 1989). Evidence suggests that a shortage of female teachers can inhibit girls' school attendance especially at the secondary level. In Kerala, for example, which has the highest female literacy and enrollment rates of all states in India, over 60 percent of the teachers are women, compared with fewer than 20 percent in the states of Bihard and Uttar Pradesh, which have the lowest female enrollment rates. The shortage of female teachers is usually worse in rural areas. Poor roads and limited public transport may especially restrict women's mobility. In Kerala, women freely travel long distances to teach in the rural schools because road transport is highly developed, safe and reliable.

Curricula and School Quality

3.19 The effect on female enrollment of curriculum and the general quality of schooling may be especially strong because parents may insist more on quality before they will pay the costs of educating girls. In some schools curricula are overloaded, irrelevant for life in the country concerned, and ineffective at teaching such essentials as mathematics and science. Girls' schools are particularly likely to lack capability in science and mathematics. Curricula in general may be heavily biased toward low-paying skills such as knitting, sewing, and secretarial work. This shortcoming has a major effect on girls' future employment opportunities as it hinders women's access to better-paying jobs. Many textbooks and other teaching materials have a pronounced sexist bias that discourages girls from thinking of themselves as good students or as suited to any but a few traditional occupations. Often books portray men as intelligent and adventurous, seeking employment in new, exciting, and profitable fields. Women are depicted as passive, admiring, and suited only for traditional roles -- if they are shown at all (Kelly and Elliott 1982). A study in Zambia found that although textbooks systematically treated men's activities as admirable, women appeared rarely and "primarily in domestic roles and were characterized as passive, stupid, and ignorant" (Hyde 1989, 34). Girls may thus receive subtle messages from textbooks that guide them into traditional roles. Aside from textbooks, if only a few years of primary schooling are offered, fewer children may be enrolled than if more complete primary or secondary schooling is offered. Fewer girls may be admitted to government secondary schools even if they are qualified, which may leave them no options except more costly and possibly poorer quality private schools. In Kenya, for instance, proportionately fewer qualified girls than boys are admitted to government-financed secondary schools, so a disproportionate number of girls attend community-based "harambee" schools cost parents more (see box 3.4).

Neglect of Girls' Health and Nutrition

3.20 Medical and anthropological research demonstrates that in much of the developing world, especially in Asia, girls are less well cared for and less nourished than boys. And it is obvious that children who are chronically hungry or ill cannot learn effectively even if they are given the chance. Of course where girls are given less opportunity to eat they are also less likely to be given an opportunity to learn -- doubling the pattern of disadvantage for girls. This pattern is strikingly evident in the abnormally low ratio of women to men (no one suggests the women emigrated) and the higher age-specific mortality rates for girls in some countries, especially in Asia.

Box 3.4 Causes and Consequences of Girls' Lower Achievement in Primary Schooling

In rural Kenya, girls' poorer performance in primary school (compared with boys) influences their lower secondary enrollment rates. Entrance to the few government secondary schools is rationed by admitting only those who pass the primary leaving examination. Even when girls graduate from the primary level, relatively few (10.6 percent in 1981 compared with 12.9 percent for boys) were admitted to the government-managed lower secondary schools. A higher proportion of qualified girls (29.1 percent) entered the unaided and lower-quality secondary or "harambee" schools compared with only 22.9 percent for boys. The harambee schools are also the alternative for students who fail. A 1982 World Bank study analyzing household level data found that girls were 17 percent less likely than boys to pass the primary leaving examination and more girls attended 'harambee' schools than government secondary schools. Since the demand for 'Harambee' school education was lower for girls than for boys, simulating a redistribution of state school places from boys to girls increased total enrollments by 15 percent for every substituted state school place.

In Cote d'Ivoire and Tanzania, rationing of school places at the secondary level by primary examination performance also lowers female access to secondary schooling. Tanzania's solution to greater female access has been to lower the pass mark for girls, but a more satisfactory longer-term solution lies in improving girls' primary achievements. This leads to the question of why fewer girls pass the primary school examination. A study in Cote d'Ivoire suggests a strong relationship between households' low economic status and girls' poor performance. Since primary education is free, opportunity costs, not direct costs, are expected to be the overriding constraint. Girls' greater involvement than boys with domestic chores may leave them too tired or with too little time to study. Moreover, the effect of positive role models for girls was significant -- girls with older sisters who passed the examination were more likely to perform well themselves.

Sources: Collier and others 1991a,b; Grisay 1984; World Bank Kenya: The Role of Women in Development 1989.

3.21 In India, for example, the sex ratio (women per thousand men) fell from 972 in 1901 to 950 in 1931 and 933 in 1981; a normal sex ratio would show at least parity for females. A.K. Sen (1987) has estimated that some 30 million Indian women are "missing" -- apparently having died prematurely. In The Lesser Child, just published by the Government of India in cooperation with UNICEF, anthropometric data from one area show retarded growth among 79 percent of female infants compared with only 43 percent in males; in children aged 1 to 2 years, the corresponding figures are 86 percent and 63 percent, and in pre-schoolers 72 percent and 65 percent, respectively. The disparity in male-female infant mortality rates is most striking in northwestern India, but even in rural Tamil Nadu, girls have a much higher incidence of all diseases and conditions except dental cavities. The Lesser Child states that "in a culture that idolizes sons and dreads the birth of a daughter, to be born female comes perilously close to being born less than human. . . Those girls who manage to survive till birth and beyond find that the dice is heavily loaded against them in a world that denies them equal access to food, health care, education, employment, and simple human dignity" (The Lesser Child, Government of India 1990 cited in SCN News (6), United Nations 1990). India is not the only country with this problem.

Low Economic Returns

3.22 As noted earlier, the opportunity costs and cultural constraints affecting girls' schooling reflect the productivity and earning capability of the current generation of women. When women earn less than men, girls are often kept home to do chores and boys are sent to school. Economic policies that constrain women's ability to earn, through self-employment or in the wage labor force, also limit the returns to female schooling and so discourage parents from educating daughters. Macroeconomic policies may protect some sectors and penalize others; disadvantaged people who cannot compete effectively may be locked into the nonprotected sectors. Legal or regulatory barriers to women's participation in the labor force or policies that effectively restrict women's access to information and resources also help perpetuate the tradition that girls stay home from school to do more chores. If cultural traditions favor female seclusion or encourage women to remain within the sphere of the home and the family while men move "outside" to earn a living, then culture and limited earning prospects may be mutually reinforcing (Kelly and Elliott 1982; World Bank Gender and Poverty in India 1991; El Sanabary 1989). Research is needed to explore the extent and severity of these intertwined cultural and economic constraints on girls' schooling.

Nature and Severity of Constraints Across Countries

3.23 The nature and severity of the constraints on girls' schooling vary, to some extent, with stage of development. While data are not adequate to firmly establish a typology, some broad patterns emerge. In poor agrarian countries (where per capita GNI is below $300), direct and opportunity costs as well as social traditions usually pose severe constraints. Female enrollments are likely to be low and the gender gap relatively wide. Much of South Asia and Africa falls into this category. For example, in Bangladesh, few families can readily afford the direct costs of schooling; a girl's opportunity cost to the family is substantial; infrastructural bottlenecks are severe; distances to schools are considerable; and female teachers are scarce. In Africa, where many women are farmers, girls may be at a particular disadvantage in secondary school because they are expected to help considerably on the farm. In both Africa and South Asia, the time required to gather fuel and water is increasing as population growth persists. Progress in female education may require an education policy that addresses several constraints simultaneously. Yet governments face severe budgetary constraints, so "combination" programs in education must be designed with great care.

3.24 The constraints in middle-income countries relate more to rural-urban differences and to labor market problems. Even in the lower middle-income countries, the constraints (such as poor infrastructure) are less severe, and education policies can promote female enrollments effectively. In Latin America, for example, female enrollments are low mainly among poor rural populations. In urban areas in some Latin American countries, progress has been dramatic.

3.25 Among middle-income countries, Middle-Eastern countries lag behind but female enrollments are catching up in all the oil-producing Arab nations. The socially less conservative countries within the region (such as Turkey and Tunisia) have far outstripped others in female education. In the rest, there are no major household or school level constraints of the kind found in the poor agrarian societies. The barriers to progress appear to be essentially sociocultural and relate to women's limited participation in the labor market. Even at higher levels of education, few places seem to go to women in science and technology, including medicine. Household-level demand-side constraints on female enrollment are weaker in the Latin American and Caribbean countries, where many women participate in the labor market.

3.26 Suitable remedial policies (such as lower costs, financial incentives, child care for siblings, satellite schools) exist to overcome these constraints. Policy can change parental attitudes toward girls' education. If policy is focused on reducing the direct and opportunity costs in a sustained manner, as well as easing other constraints (such as segmentation of the labor market), parents will increasingly educate their daughters. To what extent have Bank-assisted and other education projects incorporated specific remedies in project design? How successful have these projects been? How has thinking evolved in Bank projects on gender issues? What recent innovations in project design tried to address specific constraints? These issues are pursued in the next chapter.

CHAPTER 4. PROMISING APPROACHES FOR INCREASING FEMALE ENROLLMENT

4.01 This chapter discusses the strategies and policy options in education projects (both Bank-assisted and others) that address constraints on girls' education in primary and secondary schools. The Bank's experience is summarized at the end of the chapter, and recommendations for future action are made.

4.02 Available evidence on how to improve and expand female education is limited: "research has shown that few, if any, nations have done more than attempt to provide more access to schools for girls. No country has dealt adequately with the quality of education girls receive, the content of that education, or the structural barriers to women's full participation in social and economic life" (Kelly and Elliott 1982, 4). Whatever rigorous evidence could be found on different strategies and policy options is summarized here. Bear in mind that several different policy changes may interact to influence girls' enrollments, making it hard to determine the impact of any one policy.

Conceptualizing and Testing Alternative Strategies

4.03 Hardly any information exists on the relative costs and effects of various strategies to improve female education. These issues are discussed in this paper in terms of logic and common sense. But rigorous research on the merits of alternative approaches to improve education for all children, and certainly for girls, is sorely needed. As a start, strategies should be conceptualized to permit testing. This requires analyzing in advance what the main constraints on education are likely to be and deciding explicitly what measures should be undertaken to overcome them. Then three levels of analysis should be undertaken to show:

- What is being tried and at what costs.
- How cost-effective specific measures are in terms of enrollment, student performance, and so on.
- What education's long-term benefits are in terms of earnings, children's health, and fertility.

Where feasible, a controlled experiment can be invaluable in demonstrating costs and effects. Ideally this requires selecting a number of similar and broadly representative areas and deciding randomly which will be program and nonprogram (and ensuring that people cannot travel from one to the other). Then it is possible to compare and analyze average behavior in program and nonprogram areas. Where this approach is not practical, a modified experiment may be tried by deliberately (rather than randomly) selecting a few program and nonprogram areas, ensuring that the areas are similar and representative of the broader population. In some cases "natural experiments" may be under way, in which certain measures are already being tried. Where controlled experiments are not possible, multivariate analysis may permit reasonably accurate measurement of the impact of specific education policies, or of other influences such as parental or community characteristics. Multivariate analysis can also help show how education policies and parental and community characteristics interrelate to affect decisions about schooling. Baseline data should be collected to show which boys and girls attend school at different levels (enrollment, attainment, dropout) and to begin to illuminate the reasons why parents send or do not send their children to school (school-level characteristics and parental and community characteristics). Careful monitoring should be undertaken as innovations are instituted and tested to show precisely what is being done and at what cost. At a minimum, enrollment patterns should be traced as these innovations proceed, and the averages for boys and girls in the program and nonprogram areas should be noted. To demonstrate impact rigorously, more extensive research should be done on shorter term effects -- at least on enrollment and ideally also on performance and dropouts. It will be valuable also to undertake some longer-term research on the impact of the gains in education. Impact research in education or other fields ideally requires randomized surveys at the household level (disaggregating by gender and talking to women as well as to men) before and after programs are instituted. In education, this research should cover enrollment patterns, the costs of schooling to parents, and parents' and children's characteristics that may affect returns to or costs of schooling. Impact research also requires community-level information about what kinds of schools are supplied (specific characteristics such as scholarships, female teachers, or location of school and costs to governments and families) as well as other community characteristics that may affect returns to or costs of schooling. Information at the community level, including costs, is usually relatively easy to obtain. Household-level sample surveys are more difficult and expensive but are essential to show what really accounts for differences in the enrollment of boys and girls. Promising research is under way in Bangladesh and Morocco and should be tried as a priority in areas where female enrollment is particularly low, notably in Africa, India, and parts of the Middle East.

4.04 Analyzing the returns and constraints associated with female education in the framework of demand and supply can help to formulate clearer strategies to increase girls' schooling and clarify the case for special efforts to educate girls (see box 4.1). Current enrollment rates for boys or girls reflect parental demand for the kind of schooling that exists. Demand for that kind of schooling can be shifted and strengthened through an exogenous increase in the demand for labor or other improvements in economic opportunity that increase the returns to education, so that more parents become willing to send children to existing schools. Such changes make sending a child to school a more attractive option, thus tipping more parental decisions in favor of enrolling children even without changes in school policy. On the other hand, changing the kind of schooling supplied can also tip decisions in favor of enrolling children, by providing a better education for a given cost or the same quality of education for a lower cost. Thus enrollment rates can be increased even without changing the underlying demand. Moreover, providing a more appealing kind of schooling can over time elicit a different pattern of demand for what amounts to a different service, as with any product differentiation, accelerating the increase in enrollment rates. Finally, providing more convenient supplies of wood, water, or child care or otherwise obviating the need for children to help at home can reduce the opportunity cost of schooling, thus making education a relatively more attractive option.

Box 4.1 Demand for and Supply of Girls' Education*

The family's demand and supply curves for girls' education are presented in figure 4.1a. The demand curve (Df) is slightly unconventional because it represents the marginal return associated with another unit of education: the marginal return falls as the years of schooling increase. This return can come either as wage increases or from self-employment or home production valued by the family. The curve (Sf) gives the marginal cost to the family of producing an additional unit of education, including direct costs such as fees and opportunity costs such as forgone earnings. The demand and supply curves should both apply either to the family or to the student to ensure consistency in the analysis. The demand curve here gives the return to the family rather than to the educated individual, since the supply curve gives the cost to the family; thus the demand curve can be interpreted to mean the returns that the family captures. The demand and supply curves are in equilibrium at E1.

The demand curve can be shifted to the right through changes in economic policies, technical change, or other exogenous shocks that increase the demand for, or the productivity of, labor either in the wage labor market or outside it. A new demand curve Df' illustrates such a shift, with a resulting increase in female education because parents are willing to pay more for it (at E2).

The supply curve can be shifted to the right by reducing the direct cost of education to parents (waiving fees, providing scholarships, and so on) as Sf' illustrates. It can also be shifted to the right by reducing the opportunity cost of girls' schooling, for instance by offering child care facilities or nearby sources of fuelwood that the family would otherwise have to purchase if the daughters who normally watch siblings or fetch wood were instead allowed to go to school. The vertical distance between Sf and S'f at any point represents the value of a new subsidy to reduce the cost to parents. A new equilibrium results (with no change in the demand curve) at E3, since a given amount of education now costs less than before Sf shifted. If both demand and supply shift, girls' enrollment increases still further, with a new equilibrium at E4.

A further option is to supply something different -- to improve the quality of education so much that it in effect constitutes a new product, depicted as Sf* (see Figure 4.1b). Even if the original demand curve Df prevails, this can result in increased education for girls if the cost to parents is as shown in this diagram, with E*1. But it is quite possible that the new product -- the better schooling -- will elicit a different pattern of demand, Df*, if, for example, it is more relevant to children's employment prospects and so raises the returns to schooling. Higher quality teaching, better books and equipment, or a roof over children's heads could all be expected to improve learning and so affect productivity more, thereby increasing the returns to schooling and inducing greater demand for education, as at E*2.

On the other hand, demand and supply curves can also be conceived of from the perspective of society (see figure 4.1c). Let Ss represent the total cost of female education borne by society. Sf is part of Ss, namely the part borne by the family. The rest of the cost is borne by government and is defined as Sg = Ss - Sf. Let Ds represent the overall demand for female education on the part of society. It will also be above the family's demand curve to the extent that society captures and values the broader returns from female education such as lower fertility rates and improved health and learning for the student's own children. The equilibrium for society is shown as E*s, which implies more female schooling than families (who make the decisions) are demanding at E1. <u>If society wishes to move the family equilibrium to E*f to correspond to the social equilibrium at E*s, it has several options</u>. As shown in this graph, it can reduce the costs to the family by assuming a larger share of the costs so that the family's supply curve shifts right and the family equilibrium moves to E*f. More generally, the society can do any or all of the following:

a) Institute economic policies that increase women's earning prospects, inducing a right shift in both Ds and Df.

b) Reduce the direct costs to parents as discussed in the example depicted in the diagram, so that the government assumes an increased share of the total costs to society.

c) Reduce the opportunity costs to parents (for instance, by providing daycare, again increasing the government's share of the cost).

---

*The ideas expressed here draw heavily on Behrman 1990 and Becker 1967 especially for figure 4.1a.

d) Provide better quality schooling, thus replacing Sf by Sf* and, one hopes, inducing a stronger demand pattern Df*. If it merely uses existing resources more efficiently (which amounts to a technical change in the production function for education), then the costs for producing a given quantity of education would not change. More realistically, the costs are likely to rise somewhat, but may induce a helpful shift up in family demand.

e) Embark on "awareness campaigns" hoping to shift family demand for education enough to raise female enrollments without having to increase government subsidies or otherwise change economic policies.

Demand and supply curves can also depict likely differences for boys and girls (see figure 4.1d). For instance, if tradition and economics combine so that the opportunity cost of educating girls is higher or if families incur costs related to stricter cultural requirements for girls (such as higher quality clothing or more transportation), then the supply curve for girls (Sfg) will be higher than a similar curve for boys (Sfb). If the economic returns from girls' schooling are lower (for instance, because women face barriers in the labor market), then the demand curve for female education (Dfg) will be to the left of the demand curve for boys (Dfb), and girls will receive less schooling than boys. Elasticities should also differ.

Box Figure 4.1: Demand for and Supply of Girls' Education

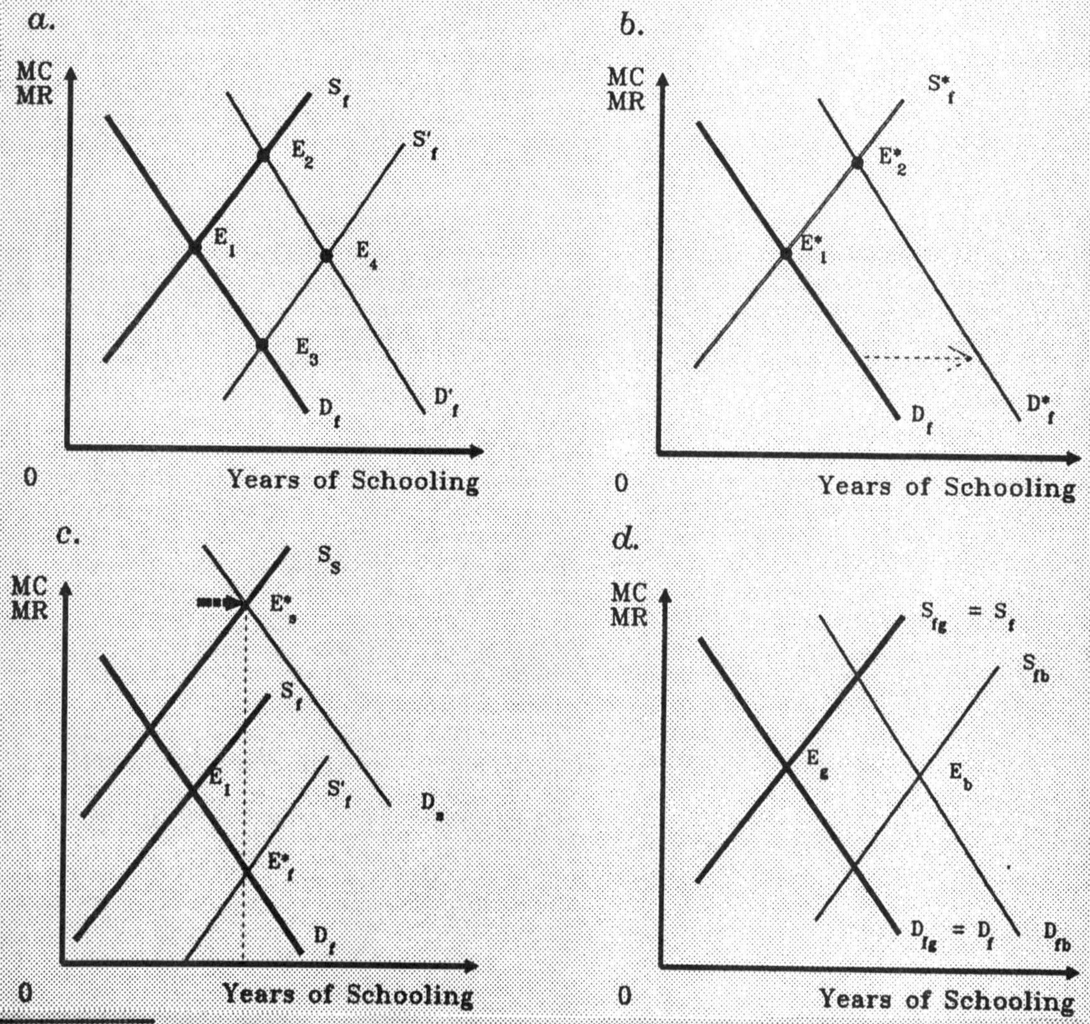

MC = Marginal Cost.
MR = Marginal Return.

A Framework for Increasing Female Education

4.05 Table 4.1 provides a framework showing how the constraints on female education suggest three categories of possible remedies: education policies, policies in other sectors that reduce the opportunity costs of girls' schooling and improve girls' health, and economic policies to improve women's earning power and so increase the returns to schooling. This chapter focuses on education policy.

4.06 The potential of macroeconomic or sectoral policies for improving women's earning capability was discussed in chapter 1. It is reasonable to expect women's earnings to rise and attitudes toward female education to shift as a result of policies to deregulate economies, strengthen the demand for labor, remove barriers to women's labor force participation, and allow women more equal access to information, resources and markets. It will then make less sense to differentiate between boys and girls at home and more sense to send all children to school. But it may take time for this process to work its way through the economy and the culture. In the meantime, education policy can be designed to deal with current economic and cultural realities in ways that tip more decisions in favor of educating girls. Measures to raise the current earning capability of women and measures to encourage girls' schooling will be mutually reinforcing.

4.07 Where culture is very restrictive and incomes are low, it will not be easy to raise girls' enrollment rates quickly or to achieve parity with boys' enrollment rates. But the evidence suggests that reasonable progress can be achieved -- and indeed it is in some of the lowest income countries and most restrictive cultures that some of the most innovative approaches to educating girls are now being tried. Over the next several years as these innovations are more widely tested, it will be crucial to evaluate them rigorously -- their costs to families and governments as well as their impacts -- and to revise policy guidance accordingly.

The Basics: Putting Schools Within Reach of Children

Expanding the Number of School Places

4.08 Expanding the number of places in school often helps to increase girls' enrollment. Children cannot go to school if too few places exist, and scarce places are often allocated first to boys. It may be sensible to reserve some school places for girls. In Malawi, for instance, the government is providing new schools, and reserves one-third of all secondary school places for girls. A Bank-assisted project to build secondary schools resulted in higher female enrollments than anticipated -- due in part to the government's policy (World Bank 1989e). Tanzania has a similar policy of reserving secondary places for girls (Cooksey and Ishumi 1986). Yet providing places is no guarantee that girls will attend; having a place is necessary but not always sufficient to overcome other constraints on female schooling, as the experience of such diverse countries as Peru, Tunisia, and Bangladesh show (Kelly and Elliott 1982; Creative Associates 1990) (see box 4.2).

Table 4.1: Constraints on Girls' School Attendance and a Framework of Approaches

A. TYPICAL CONSTRAINTS INFLUENCING PARENTAL DECISIONS:

Direct Costs	Opportunity Costs	Limited Economic Returns
For example, for fees, books, clothing, and to address cultural and safety concerns.	Chore time, sibling care, foregone earnings (girls' and mothers').	Macroeconomic policies, limited access to labor markets and resources, quality of education

B. APPROACHES TO OVERCOME CONSTRAINTS AT DIFFERENT LEVELS:

School Level - Reduce the direct and opportunity costs of schooling for girls; address access and safety concerns; and improve the quality of schooling offered:

A. For Girls	B. For All Children
1. Reservation of school places for girls	1. Expansion of school places
2. Awareness campaigns focused on girls	2. Closer schools with regular teachers
3. Incentives (e.g. scholarships) or fees waived only for girls	3. Compulsory education and awareness campaigns
4. Girls' schools	4. Reduced fees or provision of free books or food
5. In coeducational schools, separate toilets and facilities for privacy (e.g. boundary walls)	5. Enhanced quality and more relevant school curriculum
6. More female teachers	6. Flexible schedules and hours
7. Child care	7. Parental/community involvement in school managment
	8. Non-formal education programs for parents

Community Level - Reduce the direct and opportunity concerns and address safety concerns:

1. Provision of wood and water supplies
2. Child care
3. Public transport

National Level - Policies to raise women's economic returns to schooling:

1. Remove macro policy distortions affecting the sectors in which women predominate
2. Ease barriers to female labor force participation
3. Increase access to information, credit, and resources for self-employed women (farmers or entrepreneurs)
4. Improve health care, nutrition, and food supplies for girls to increase learning ability.

Box 4.2 Effects of Expanding the School System in Peru

In Peru over the past 50 years, the government carried out a campaign to expand the school system and increase enrollments sharply and expanded the education system in the mid 1950s and 1960s. In 1940, males averaged 2.4 years of schooling and females 1.4. By 1981, males had 6.7 years of schooling and females 5.4 years. Girls' enrollment rates increased from 65 percent in 1955 to 99 percent by 1970, a larger gain than boys made because more boys had been enrolled earlier. Progress was faster for women in urban areas.

Using the number of grades to show the overall availability of schooling, the number of grades improves enrollment especially among more recent age cohorts. For males born before 1940, adding a grade increased school attainment by half a year, compared with 1.3 years for males born in the 1960's. A similar but later increase occurs for women, showing that the initial impact of increasing the supply of schooling was to worsen inequality between men and women. As primary schools became more available, the quality of schooling was also improved -- for instance by adding textbooks, which has about twice as much impact for girls (adding about .7 years) as for boys (.3 years) in the cohort born in 1960-66. (The number of teachers per school, holding constant for number of grades, seemed to matter less consistently but was significant for boys and girls in some cohorts.) These results suggest that a shortage of school places constrained enrollment in the earlier years and that -- when school expansion is combined with an effort to assure that schools have books and teachers -- female and male enrollments can be increased and the gender gap can be narrowed. Parental education also influenced the enrollment rates of older cohorts, although it had less influence as schools were expanded and improved. Maternal and paternal education both promoted daughter's schooling. Maternal education mattered more for daughters, while father's education mattered more for sons. Mother's and father's employment also boosted a daughter's education (more than a son's).

Source: King and Bellew 1991 in Herz and Khandker 1991.

4.09 Expansion in school places can be financed in two ways. First, public and private education spending can be increased by raising the overall budget, reallocating in favor of education, or instituting carefully designed cost-recovery to avoid penalizing girls at least through the secondary level. Second, internal efficiency can be improved (which increases the availability of places by reducing dropouts and repetition). Given the fiscal crunch in many developing countries, improving efficiency may often be more feasible than increasing total spending on education (see, for example, World Bank Primary Education Policy Paper 1990). But there is a problem. Although reducing the number of dropouts theoretically benefits girls more than boys because more girls drop out of school, it is usually harder to reduce the number of female dropouts because of the special barriers to education that girls face. Achieving greater internal efficiency is easier said than done. It requires addressing the constraints on girls' education.

Reducing the Distance to School

4.10 In increasing the number of school places, it is logical to consider the school system's organizational structure: will the emphasis be on a few large, centralized schools that offer a broad range of programs or on a network of many small schools, even one-room schoolhouses with closer ties to the community but less scope for a broad range of programs? Opting for schools closer to children's homes will particularly promote the enrollment of girls, because of parental concern about girls' safety and social reputations (World Bank Primary Education Policy Paper 1990; Stromquist 1987; World Bank Bangladesh: Strategies for Enhancing the Role of Women in Development 1990; World Bank Gender and Poverty in India 1991; World Bank Women in Pakistan 1989; Lavy forthcoming). Fortunately, research suggests that smaller schools with closer ties to the community are more effective for boys as well as girls so there is no essential conflict between short distances and effectiveness.

4.11 But networks of small schools do pose the management and administrative problems commonly associated with decentralization. When personnel and facilities are widely dispersed, supervision, communication, and logistics are typically hard to manage: distant central authorities must keep in touch with many more local points. Evidence from health and family planning programs as well as from education suggests, however, that community involvement can substitute for some central supervision, and community involvement is easier to achieve with local service points. Local involvement can be supplemented by periodic assessments and visits from more senior central authorities to promote quality control and comparable services. Increased local involvement may also generate better ideas for improving the quality of education and other practical contributions such as the help building schools that occurred in Kenya (World Bank Kenya: The Role of Women in Development 1989). Communities may be more willing and better able to help build smaller schools with less complex architecture. Then governments can concentrate more on providing or training teachers, furnishing equipment, and maintaining overall standards of quality and student and teacher performance.

4.12 Countries have approached the distance problem in two ways: by bringing schools closer to homes and by providing boarding facilities so girls can attend distant schools (see box 4.3). Innovative "cluster" or "satellite schools" appear to be an inexpensive and feasible way to locate schools closer to the community, especially at the primary level. Such an approach proved successful in Bangladesh where "satellite" schools comprising the first two or three primary grades were located in the community and supervised by a more distant main primary school. These schools operated with flexible hours to allow children chore-time. Once the girls became accustomed to attending the first few grades at the satellite schools, they (and their parents) were more willing to continue at the more distant upper primary schools. Research shows that when a community also has a secondary school nearby, parents may be more willing to let children start primary school because they want them to reach the secondary level where they believe the benefits really lie (Lavy, forthcoming). So Morocco is providing more small local schools for middle-level education under a new Bank-assisted project. The evidence on boarding is more mixed: boarding may be required where populations are dispersed or nomadic, but is likely to be expensive. A third approach may be multigrade teaching. A Bank-assisted project in The Gambia is introducing multigrade teaching in rural primary schools where classes are too small to warrant one teacher per class. This practice will be extended as primary education expands. More experimental projects along these lines are needed to allow firm conclusions on the cost-effectiveness of different ways to deal with distance.

Measures to Build Parental Motivation and Cut Costs to Families

Awareness Campaigns, Community Involvement, and Compulsory Education

4.13 Parental attitudes may change as opportunity or direct costs fall, but in the meantime awareness campaigns, community involvement programs, and compulsory education laws may also affect social norms. These three types of measures tend to be mutually reinforcing. Awareness campaigns and community involvement are not likely to cost much financially or politically; enforcement of compulsory education laws may be a more delicate question. It is often common sense to enlist the support of leaders in different fields to encourage parents to send both boys and girls to school. While no econometric evidence exists on the separate impact of awareness campaigns, China seems to have done remarkably well in raising girls' enrollment, and awareness campaigns have been an important feature of Chinese education policy (see box 4.4). At the same time, parents ought to be given the opportunity for involvement in their children's education, to permit consideration of their views on what is taught and how and to encourage local contributions of ideas, resources, and management.

Box 4.3 Relieving the Distance Constraint: More Local Schools and Boarding

Parents' concerns about girls' safety, social reputations, and time away from work at home makes distance a stronger deterrent to girls' enrollment than to boys'. Two measures have been tried to address the distance constraint: providing boarding schools and locating schools closer to girls' homes.

One of the earliest experiments was to provide boarding. The results were mixed. In Malawi, additional boarding places for girls' schools were provided under an early Bank-assisted project after evidence revealed that over 90 percent of girls in boarding schools completed secondary school, compared to only 10 percent of girls enrolled in day schools. Enrollments in the project facilities doubled, but female enrollments in day schools fell by two-thirds. Overall, the proportion of female enrollments rose only 0.5 percent as places previously held by girls in the day schools were occupied by boys. The experiment proved expensive too. Despite the evidence pointing to girls' better performance in boarding schools and the heavy demand for boarding facilities found in the project audit, the government has focused on day schools in subsequent projects, because of cost constraints. It is not clear from the Malawi experiment whether girls from relatively poorer segments of society were attracted to boarding schools. Considering that girls in poor families have to perform more chores, the boarding option may not be as attractive to poorer families as to relatively well-off parents. The latter may prefer boarding schools for reasons other than distance, such as better quality of education.

Locating schools closer to children's homes seems generally more promising, especially when combined with other measures to improve the appeal of schooling, as Bangladesh's experience illustrates. Introduced in 1985 by a nongovernment organization (NGO), the "satellite" schools experiment in Bangladesh was an innovative way to bring schools closer to girls: two or three schools comprising at least the first three primary grades were located closer to the community and supervised by the relatively distant main primary school. The satellite schools operated only 2 1/2 hours a day with a predominantly female teaching force, and school schedules were chosen to accommodate rural children's work. As a result, participation rates were greater than anticipated: girls comprised 63 percent of the enrollments and fewer than 1 percent dropped out. Further, 87 percent of girls went on to continue their education at government primary schools. Based on the success of the satellite schools, a recent Bank-financed project will help the Bangladesh government open 200 such rural schools.

The Government of Bhutan is also introducing extended classrooms (ECRs) consisting of the lower primary grades clustered around the main primary schools. Female enrollment is expected to rise because the ECRs eliminate the need for walking long distances or for boarding schools at the lower grades. Girls are also expected to continue their studies as boarding will be provided at the upper primary level.

It may be sensible to concentrate the new schools in areas of greatest female underrepresentation. Ongoing projects in Pakistan and Morocco are using school mapping techniques to establish criteria for targeting new schools in currently underserved areas. Morocco's strategy is to have smaller and therefore more secondary schools in rural areas. In Pakistan's Sindh province, girls' primary schools will be located within 1.5 km. of a community compared with 2.5 km. for boys' schools.

Sources: Begum and others 1988 in Bellew and King 1991; World Bank 1975a; 1983a; 1988a; 1990h; 1990l; 1991b.

Decentralization of decision-making on education in China led to several innovative policies to improve girls' schooling, which included many successful leadership campaigns (some involving prizes) at the community level. Literacy programs for parents, especially mothers, may also complement the awareness campaigns by building motivation to allow girls to attend school. For instance, research in Africa shows that maternal education affects girls' enrollment in Côte d'Ivoire and Ghana; and experience with literacy classes in Kenya, Ethiopia, Zambia, and Zimbabwe has shown female participants to be numerous or even in the majority (Lavy forthcoming; Collier and others 1991a,b; Abadzi and others 1989 in King and Hill 1991). Several countries now provide "community rooms" in new schools where adult literacy and other programs can be held.

4.14 In some 130 countries, schooling is compulsory; enforcement of compulsory education laws varies widely but is usually weak. There is no evidence on the impact of separate decisions to make schooling compulsory, and there has been little systematic analysis of efforts to enforce compulsory schooling. This may be because compulsory education policies cannot be expected to work unless, at a minimum, schools are available and affordable for families. Thus, leadership campaigns and policy changes to make schooling compulsory are often combined with efforts to expand school places, encourage local participation, and reduce costs to parents.

Box 4.4 **Awareness Campaigns to Promote Female Education**

Parental attitudes towards girls' schooling in a given cultural setting are in part rational responses to the prevailing situation: low quality or poor relevance of school services; lack of earning opportunities for women in the labor force; and concerns about girls' safety. Yet social norms opposing female education can reduce demand for girls' schooling even further. The ultimate solution lies in changing the situation: measures to improve the quality and relevance of education; interventions to ensure the safety of girls; and labor market reforms to improve economic returns to female education. In the interim, community campaigns may be helpful in encouraging a shift of social norms to favor more equal education for boys and girls.

Awareness campaigns aimed at parents and the community to raise female enrollment have been tried. For instance, China's Gansu province conducted informational campaigns and distributed publicity materials encouraging parents to enroll their children in school and explaining the compulsory education law. A special effort to raise female enrollment was made with the assistance of religious leaders in minority areas and campaigns through the Women's Federation. It is difficult to know how much effect the awareness campaigns have had, but these efforts appear to have helped in achieving the target of 43 percent female primary enrollment in 1989 from 40 percent in 1986, and in surpassing the target for female secondary school enrollment. In Morocco, as part of an ongoing Bank-assisted project, promotional campaigns stressing the benefits of female education to families and communities are held in villages that get new schools. Preliminary data suggest an increase of 5 percent in girls' Grade 1 enrollments since the campaigns started in 1989 which may be due to the campaigns or other factors such as the provision of more schools. Similar campaigns aimed at raising female primary enrollments are in the planning stages or currently underway in Ethiopia, Mali, Nigeria, Pakistan, and Papua New Guinea.

Community involvement appears to be the key to successful identification and implementation of awareness campaigns. An early Bank-financed project in Papua New Guinea that helped raise female enrollment involved prominent community members in monitoring absenteeism and encouraging female participation. In Hunan province, China, one village sponsored a "Girls' School Attendance" award funded by local contributions after which girls' enrollments reached 100 percent. In recent Bank projects in Morocco and Bangladesh, community involvement in primary education is encouraged along with local initiatives to make schools more attractive to girls.

Sources: Kleynhoff 1991; Lockheed and Verspoor 1991; Searle 1989; UNESCO 1987a, 1987b; World Bank 1989f, 1989h; 1990d, 1990h, 1990k, 1990l.

Reducing the Direct Costs of Schooling

4.15 Empirical evidence on the importance of reducing the direct costs of schooling (tuition, textbooks, such school inputs as uniforms, and transport) is also limited. The direct costs are known to account for 5 to 10 percent of household consumption in families in many developing countries, and as much as 20 percent in some poor families (World Bank 1990o; World Bank Primary Education Policy Paper 1990; World Bank Women in Pakistan 1989). If poor families now send most boys to school at least for a few years but consider schooling for girls more expensive and less likely to benefit the family, then reducing the direct costs of schooling for all children equally may raise girls' enrollments more than those of boys.

4.16 Educational policies often combine awareness campaigns and laws to make education compulsory with measures to reduce costs. Examples include China, Korea, and Sri Lanka, -- countries where female enrollments are now strikingly high. In Korea, compulsory education was combined with such incentives for disadvantaged students as the waiving of fees, the provision of free textbooks and school meals, and reduced uniform costs (UNESCO 1984a). Sri Lanka has offered free textbooks for all students, scholarships for students from needy families, school feeding programs at the lower primary level, and alternative school structures to supplement its policy of compulsory education (UNESCO 1984b). China's national compulsory education law of 1986, in addition to requiring all children aged 6 to attend school, waives tuition for all students and makes stipends available to needy children (see box 4.5 on China). No econometric studies could be found to identify the precise impact of these policy measures. But enrollment rates for both boys and girls have risen since these policies were instituted and compare favorably to enrollment rates for countries of similar per capita GNI.

Box 4.5 China's Experience in Raising Enrollments

The decentralization of primary education and cost reduction have played an important role in China's achieving close to universal primary education (UPE) despite its low per capita income. Several provinces introduced compulsory educations laws prior to the nine-year compulsory education law approved by the National People's Congress in 1986. Policy measures to raise primary enrollments, especially of girls, have been devised at the local level in response to local constraints. The programs have included: campaigns to motivate parents to enroll their children (involving religious leaders and the Women's Federation); active community support in encouraging the enrollment of all children; a responsibility system whereby principals and teachers encourage enrollment and retention; alternative structures of primary education (including flexible scheduling, night classes and part-work, part-study programs); financial assistance in the form of waiving of tuition and other school fees (including pupil and textbook fees); the provision of monthly stipends; special schools for girls; and sibling care. These measures have significantly contributed to raising girls' primary enrollments, especially in the poor rural and mountainous areas.

Sources: Coletta and Sutton 1990; Searle 1989; UNESCO 1984c, 1987b.

4.17 In contrast, Kenya's experience shows the importance of doing more than removing tuition requirements. Following the introduction of free education in 1974, grade 1 enrollments in Kenya increased by 145 percent for boys and 161 percent for girls. However, the direct costs to parents of schooling subsequently increased because communities were allowed to impose additional fees, such as building levies and student activity fees. The fees quadrupled the cost of education in some districts. Dropout rates increased and were higher in poorer districts (Nkinyangi 1982). The negative response of parents to rising costs is reflected in recent survey results from Kenya's Kisumu District which revealed that 40 percent of primary school dropouts are attributable to the high direct costs of schooling (World Bank 1991e).

Special Incentives and Scholarships for Girls

4.18 A further possibility is to reduce the costs for girls more than for boys through special scholarships or the waiving of fees only for girls. These programs can be costly, but the subsidies can be justified on the grounds of the greater social benefits of girls' education. There is evidence of a substantial increase in girls' enrollment, but caution is needed because subsidies can be misdirected. In a Bank-assisted project in Bangladesh, for example, some uniforms went to ineligible girls. The program was discontinued and scholarships were instituted instead (see box 4.6). Scholarship programs can be made practical and effective. Close cooperation with the community, careful identification of target groups, and "tying" the scholarships to the student concerned or waiving fees as distinct from providing a commodity such as clothing (which can be resold) can help ensure that scholarships work as intended. Building on the experience of past programs, a Bank-financed project is currently expanding the scholarship effort in Bangladesh and incorporating other measures to reduce the direct costs to parents of girls' schooling.

Box 4.6 Scholarships for Girls: Country Experience

Bangladesh's Secondary Education Scholarship Program gave over 18,000 girls in grades 6-10 scholarships to cover secondary school tuition. Initiated in 1977, the project has succeeded in almost doubling female secondary school enrollments -- from 27.3 percent of eligible girls before the project, to 43.5 percent after project intervention. The number of female dropouts over the same period has also decreased substantially in the project area, from 14.7 to 3.5 percent. Moreover, the possibility of receiving a scholarship in grade 6 has led to increased female attendance in the lower primary school grades in program areas. Important lessons learned include the necessity of establishing realistic selection criteria for students receiving scholarships and the need to build these into the project at the beginning. The decision to limit funding to a target group of girls from "poor" families after the project was under way proved unwise as: a) the chosen indicator of poverty was too low; b) administrative costs increased and school places were left empty because of problems identifying suitable candidates; and c) community support deteriorated when some girls were excluded.

Despite these problems, the program met its main goal: female graduates "are marrying later, bearing fewer children, finding employment outside the home, and in some cases, working outside their natal region", all of which point to considerable change in cultural attitudes (Creative Associates 1990, 2). The Government of Bangladesh recently announced a policy of free secondary education for girls up to grade 8.

Guatemala's scholarship program for primary school girls began in 1987 in a rural Indian community where only 53 percent of girls were enrolled in primary school and the completion rate was 17 percent. The selection of female recipients in this program, unlike the Bangladesh program, is carried out by parents' committees from the outset. Priority is given to those girls who had never attended school and those deemed most needy. Monthly stipends are allocated for each girl as long as she remains in school. Verification of the girls' attendance and payments are supervised by a local woman, and girls who do not pass a grade are given tutoring assistance. The 11 communities in the program are visited by a social worker twice a month, have training sessions for parents monthly, and hold annual evaluation meetings.

The program has shown remarkable success in enrolling and retaining girls: over 90 percent of the scholarship girls completed the first year. Of the 1,500 beneficiaries over the 3-year life of the project, only 5 girls have dropped out, "due to extenuating circumstances during a teachers' strike" (Creative Associates 1990, 4). The involvement of community groups in the targeting process and monitoring of the program has been instrumental in its success. One unanticipated problem is that girls completing their primary education have been encouraged to continue with secondary education, yet existing post-primary schools are located far from the communities. The distance problem constrains the further education of these girls' as boarding is prohibitively expensive and not culturally acceptable.

Sources: Bellew and King 1991; Creative Associates 1990; World Bank 1990h.

Improving the Quality of Schooling

4.19 It is logical to expect that the type of schooling offered also affects parental willingness to incur the costs of education. Parents in any country will naturally be concerned with the relevance of education, the quality of teaching, and the regular attendance of the teacher. Parents in many countries may also prefer that education be offered in ways that suit current cultural constraints on girls. Having a school nearby helps, of course. But cultural requirements may also mean that girls need separate lavatories, or separate schools, or female teachers.

Providing a Relevant Curriculum, Textbooks, and Other Basics

4.20 Research has established that once schools are basically in place, incremental investment in physical infrastructure is less important for students' learning than incremental expenditures on curriculum design, textbooks, and other inputs to improve school quality (Armitage and others 1986; Harbison and Hanushek, forthcoming; Lockheed and Verspoor 1991). Of course, providing free textbooks or other materials is essentially a way of reducing costs -- but it also helps to make education services comparable overall. Evidence suggests that parents are more willing to educate boys and girls if they find the curriculum relevant and the quality of schooling adequate. Curricula should be streamlined to avoid or reduce overload from non-essentials and to focus on the main priorities, including mathematics and science, for girls as well as boys (Lockheed and Verspoor 1991). In almost every country women study less mathematics and science than men (see, for example, Jimenez and Lockheed 1989). Substantial research shows that this reflects a subtle interaction between traditional attitudes on what women "should study" and the options for study offered to women and girls. Girls' schools often lack the same offerings in mathematics or science (or the same equipment) as for boys, and even teachers may discourage girls from studying these subjects. Yet mathematics and science are especially important to improve economic productivity and promote competitiveness in modern economies and to improve children's health and learning.

4.21 If girls can be offered more science and mathematics and encouraged to study these subjects, the benefits should be substantial (for nontraditional or traditional occupations) and some parents may be willing to finance more education for their daughters. In Kenya, for instance, where proportionately fewer qualified girls than boys gain admission to government schools, parents spend more to send girls to private secondary schools. Three times as many of these girls study science as do girls in the less costly government schools, suggesting that parents are more willing to pay if girls can study science (World Bank Kenya: The Role of Women in Development 1989).

4.22 The quality of schooling is likely to matter particularly for girls because parents have more doubts about education for girls. In Peru, when free textbooks were supplied to primary schools, girls were 1.3 times more likely to enroll, whereas no effect was recorded for boys' enrollments (King and Bellew 1991 in Herz and Khandker 1991). Thus efforts such as "Operation Blackboard" in India may help girls even more than boys. "Operation Blackboard" is meant to provide essential facilities to all primary schools in India, including classrooms, toilets, blackboards, books, and learning materials; all single-teacher schools will gain at least one more teacher, preferably a woman, and teacher training will be improved (World Bank Gender and Poverty in India 1991). A Bank-assisted project in Morocco provides subsidized textbooks for about 15 percent of primary school students in rural areas. A companion project plans to build on this experience to supply low-cost textbooks to upper-basic students in rural areas. One Bank-assisted project in Pakistan offers free textbooks for primary school girls and scholarships for secondary school girls in the Sindh province. Other examples of inputs were noted earlier as part of broader efforts to cut costs. Care should be taken to ensure that textbooks do not promote a sexist bias that discourages girls from learning or that limits girls' aspirations. The quality of schooling for both genders may also be increased by reducing gender-based stereotyping in curricula and teaching materials and by showing women as well as men in nontraditional and varied roles. In Zimbabwe a government policy was introduced in 1985 to eliminate sex-stereotyping in teaching materials (World Bank Zimbabwe WID Strategy draft report 1991). In Mexico, gender stereotypes depicting women in traditional roles are being removed from textbooks (Bustillo 1989); Costa Rica has designed textbooks to include positive female roles (Lockheed and Verspoor, 1991); and Guatemala has begun a major effort to modify its textbooks (Winter 1991). Bank-assisted projects in Bangladesh and The Gambia support the development of unbiased education materials and teacher training programs designed to eliminate gender-bias in the classroom.

4.23 Many countries are also aware of gender streaming in secondary schools where girls are expected to study arts, and boys science subjects, and some are implementing policies to remedy this situation. For example, a Bank-assisted project in Tanzania is promoting mathematics and science courses in new secondary schools, where about 60 percent of the facilities added will be for girls' schools. The Government of Kenya, under a Bank-assisted project, is improving science equipment in 600 schools: 300 coeducational schools, 200 girls' and 100 boys' schools. The Government of The Gambia has decided to increase the number of female teachers in traditionally male-dominated subjects, such as science and mathematics, and is actively encouraging girls to enroll in these classes.

4.24 In some places -- for example, Mali -- girls have been encouraged to attend mosque or Koranic schools, which offer greater protection because of the presence of a religious instructor. In Mali, Koranic schools appear to have raised girls' enrollments. Girls constitute 47 percent of primary enrollments in Koranic schools compared with 32 percent in government primary schools. In Pakistan, however, girls' enrollment in mosque schools has been even lower than in government primary schools (Bellew and King 1991). This may be because parents perceive the quality of education being offered there as poor.

4.25 In many developing countries the traditional practice of early marriage and the importance of preserving girls' social reputations leads to heavy dropouts at the onset of puberty, and some school policies exacerbate this problem by not allowing girls to attend class when they are pregnant or have children. In Malawi a girl is expelled from the school system when pregnant, for example (World Bank 1990n). In Nigeria, however, Kaduna state offers one year of maternity leave for young mothers (World Bank 1990k). Other projects offer child care for siblings or girls' own children (see below). A recent Bank-assisted project in The Gambia lowers the school entry age for girls from 8 years to 6, which should help girls gain more years of education before they reach marriageable age (World Bank 1990i). Education about family life is also being introduced in various countries, including the Gambia, Kenya, and Zimbabwe.

Providing Facilities for Girls

4.26 In building schools, a critical minimum of physical infrastructure appears to be needed to attract and retain girls at school. Girls usually require separate lavatories, and in cultures where male-female contact is strictly limited, girls may need separate times for using eating facilities. They may also prefer separate schools or separate boarding facilities or walls around their schools. Lack of such physical facilities may discourage girls proportionately more than boys. A few ongoing projects have recognized this need and provide for the required infrastructure. For example, two ongoing projects in Pakistan provide boundary walls, toilets, and wells for girls' and mixed schools and special attention to the design and construction of new girls' schools. Current projects in Bangladesh and Morocco also provide for latrines and tubewells in primary and secondary schools, which should increase enrollments particularly of girls.

Establishing More Girls' Schools

4.27 Experience also suggests that single-sex schools rather than coeducational schools may help to increase female enrollments and may have more positive effects on girls' achievement and self-perceptions (see box 4.7) (Jimenez and Lockheed 1989). Even in cultures practicing female seclusion, some parents may be willing to send girls to coeducational schools for a few years, but having girls' schools available can be important once girls reach puberty (see, for example, Kelly and Elliott 1982). Moreover, single-sex education apparently promotes girls' attendance and performance in a wide variety of cultures. Research from several countries shows that girls tend to perform better in a variety of subjects ranging from language to mathematics if they attend girls' schools, especially at the secondary level (Jimenez and Lockheed 1989). It is difficult to attribute these effects to school characteristics alone, because nonschool factors such as socioeconomic background, ability, and motivation may affect both the choice of school and educational outcomes. What coeducational or single-sex schools actually do differently is not well understood, but research now emerging sheds more light on these questions. Some evidence suggests that girls have greater opportunity to learn and more encouragement to excel and to try nontraditional subjects from both teachers and peers in a girls' school. A study in Thailand, for example, shows that girls in single-sex schools do substantially better than girls in coeducational schools, after taking account of possible selection bias and background factors (though boys seem to do better in coeducational environments in this study). Failure to correct for selection bias would underestimate the benefits of girls' schools. "Peer effects" seem to account for many of the benefits of single-sex education for girls (Jimenez and Lockheed 1989). Research on countries of disparate socioeconomic circumstances confirms the gist of these findings (Lee and Lockheed 1990).

Box 4.7 Girls' Schools in Kenya

Kenya's "O level" examinations after form IV determine who can go on to form V. According to data available from 1984-85, girls constituted only 38 percent of all students who took the "O level" examinations, but almost half of those who failed were girls. But girls who were enrolled in girls' schools performed much better: 6 out of the 10 leading secondary schools (as judged by examination performance) were girls' schools. The data below illustrate girls' improved performance in single-sex schools.

Kenya Certificate of Education, 1981
(percentage passes)

Subject	Grade	Girls in Girls' Schools	Boys in Boys' Schools	Girls in Mixed Schools	Boys in Mixed Schools
English	A	3.2	1.6	0.7	0.8
	B	35.2	30.0	19.3	16.8
	C	38.1	37.9	30.2	29.2
	D	23.5	30.5	49.8	52.2
Mathematics	A	1.6	4.2	0.5	2.4
	B	5.9	30.7	8.7	16.6
	C	20.7	23.0	12.1	17.3
	D	61.8	42.1	78.7	63.7
Physics	A	0.2	6.1	0	0
	B	32.4	39.5	9.0	26.1
	C	35.4	32.2	42.4	39.5
	D	31.8	24.0	48.4	34.2

In the more advanced "A level" examinations, about one-fourth of the candidates were girls, and more than a third of the girls achieved high grades. About 8 percent of boys compared to 4 percent of girls failed -- probably reflecting stronger selection bias among the girls. Recent reports from the Government of Kenya suggest that girls now outperform boys at the "O level," too. Research is needed to explain why, as this would have implications for other African countries.

Source: Eshiwani 1985 in World Bank Kenya: The Role of Women in Development 1989.

Recruiting More Female Teachers

4.28 In sociocultural settings where male-female contact is strictly limited, evidence suggests that recruitment of female teachers enhances girls' enrollment. It is difficult to establish causality between female teachers and female enrollment, but international cross-section data suggest some positive correlation between enrollment parity (girls per 100 boys) and the proportion of female teachers (see figure 4.2 below). This association is not weakened even when data are truncated by regions or limited to comparable income levels, suggesting the possible importance of female teachers in all sociocultural settings.

Figure 4.2: Proportion of Women Teachers & Female/Male Ratio in Secondary School

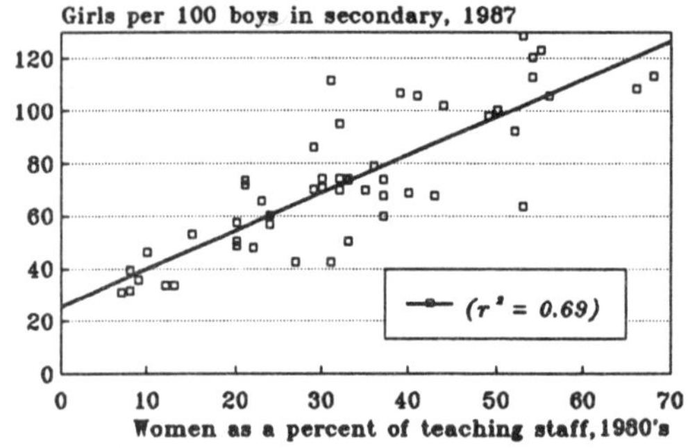

Source: Unesco 1991

4.29 The same cultural constraints that require girls to be taught by women often make it difficult to attract women to rural teaching posts. The shortage of female teachers is much greater in rural areas. Some countries -- for example, Morocco, Somalia, and Yemen -- have a surplus of both male and female teachers in urban areas, but an acute shortage in rural areas. As a first step, it makes sense to ensure that the salary system for teachers is not biased against rural posting. In Cameroon, for example, teachers are given a special bonus for urban posting (Bellew and King 1991). To increase the proportion of female teachers substantially, especially in rural areas, innovative recruitment and teacher training policies may also be needed. Policies tried by various countries include targets for women's recruitment, broadening the pool of potential teachers by removing age restrictions and modifying formal education requirements for women, focusing recruitment of rural teachers on women from local areas who are willing to serve there, and providing teachers with housing and transportation. Simply providing housing may not be enough, as experience in Pakistan has shown (World Bank, 1990f). In Nepal, a more comprehensive approach has worked: it offered home-posting for women teachers, lowered entry requirements for some rural girls, subsidized their secondary education, and supported girls through conventional teacher training with a monthly stipend, travel expenses, medical care, and tutoring. Community involvement was important: an intensive community awareness campaign preceded the teacher training program in Nepal (see Box 4.8). The number of female teachers increased and after that female school enrollments improved. In Yemen, teacher training has been the principal policy to increase female enrollments over the last 15 years, and in a current Bank-assisted project the government is considering maternity and long-leave policies for female teachers to allow easy re-entry (see box 4.8). In Pakistan's Baluchistan province, providing buses for female teachers proved a practical way to transport them to distant schools (Government of Baluchistan 1991).

4.30 Bangladesh is making a major effort to promote female teacher recruitment through a Bank-assisted project. The project design provides that 60 percent of new teachers must be female and that salary costs will be financed under the Bank project for these women teachers; the government is expected to bear the salary costs for men employed as teachers.

4.31 Evidence from Bangladesh and Pakistan suggests that it is possible to find good female teachers to serve rural areas by easing formal educational requirements, providing training, and posting women teachers near their homes. Women may be hired as assistant teachers, with less formal qualifications for teaching but more aptitude and motivation. Teachers with lower formal qualifications may be restricted to teaching the lower primary grades, but in-service teacher training can give them a chance to upgrade their skills. A Bank-financed project in Pakistan contains a component for in-service training of less qualified teachers; 15,000 of the 17,500 teachers to be trained under the project are women. Research indicates that teachers' knowledge of subject matter is more important to children's learning than formal qualifications or experience, which are the traditional quality indicators (Hanushek and Harbison, forthcoming). Thus, the combination of motivated female assistant teachers (who have a stake in the village where they are settled) and active in-service training and supervision may provide a suitable solution to the shortage of female teachers in some rural areas. An ongoing Bank-assisted project in China aims to raise female participation in in-service teacher training programs. An active recruitment campaign for female teachers is planned, along with the provision of day-care facilities at some correspondence centers.

4.32 Measures to promote recruitment of and training for female teachers may carry more additional costs than similar efforts for male teachers. On the other hand, salary savings may be achieved through greater use of assistant teachers, and special measures may be targeted to the most underserved areas. Reduced absenteeism and greater commitment from locally hired teachers may also enhance cost-effectiveness. Using a network of many local assistant teachers may accentuate the issues of administration and supervision associated with decentralization already arising in the choice of a system of many small schools. Yet top-down management has often proved problematic, and the local-school, local-teacher option may be more conducive to effective local management, perhaps supplemented by some central system of visits and assessments to promote quality control.

Reducing the Opportunity Costs: Obviating or Facilitating Girls' Chores

4.33 Particularly for poor families, it is important to reduce the opportunity costs of girls' schooling as much as possible. This involves recognizing that under present circumstances, parents rely heavily on girls' labor for household chores. Opportunity costs may be reduced either by obviating the need for so much chore time for girls or by designing education policy to allow girls more opportunity to learn while enabling them to perform at least some of their household chores. This double burden of school and substantial chore time is hardly ideal, but it may be a practical necessity as a start. As economic circumstances change to increase women's earning capability, the returns to female education will rise and traditions requiring girls to do more chores than boys may change. In the meantime, providing more flexible school hours, establishing child care facilities, and improving the community's supplies of wood and water can all help decrease the opportunity cost of sending girls to school. Box 4.9 suggests specific ways that have been tried. For example, in Pune, India, providing flexible school hours through nonformal education was key to drawing working children, especially girls, into primary school. Part-time and flexible scheduling has also been implemented with success in several provinces in China. Experiments with flexible scheduling are now taking place in Bank-financed projects in Bangladesh, Morocco, and Pakistan.

Box 4.8 Strategies to Increase the Supply of Female Teachers: Country Experience

With UNESCO and other donor assistance, Nepal began an innovative program in 1971 involving a number of policy measures to address simultaneously various constraints on rural girls' access to teacher training. Awareness campaigns, community involvement, financial assistance, tutoring, and home-posting supplemented by in-service training were offered to address cultural attitudes about the education of girls, economic constraints, and the opportunity costs of attending school. To address the low educational levels of rural girls in the very areas where female teachers were recruited, an upgrading program allowed girls from villages without secondary schools to enroll in courses leading to teacher training. In eight years (1972-80), the percentage of females in the primary school teaching force grew from 3 to 10 percent, with trainees accounting for more than a quarter of new female teachers. The measures of "positive discrimination" in the project helped equalize opportunities for girls. Awareness of the economic and social value of education for girls helped change prevailing attitudes. The more than tenfold increase in girls' primary enrollments during this period compares favorably with the increase in female teachers. A UNESCO evaluation of the project revealed that, on average, female primary enrollment and retention rates were higher in schools taught by project teachers than in the district or the nation.

A similar program containing multiple incentives for rural female teacher trainees has been operating in Yemen since 1987 with assistance from UNICEF. The project targeted rural girls who had completed grade 6. To address the lack of facilities in rural areas, primary teacher training colleges were started in existing secondary institutions close to girls' homes. Transportation by bus to and from classes was provided, along with a monthly stipend. After the 2-year training period, the program moved to other rural areas. The success of the pilot project is indicated by the low dropout rate, less than 1.5 percent, among the initial 80 female students over the course of the program even though several married during training.

Several Bank projects in Yemen have addressed the need to train more female teachers especially to attract students from rural areas, but the results were mixed presumably for lack of sensitivity to cultural constraints. For example, experiments with double shifting for girls' in boys' training institutes failed because of the presence of male boarders on campus during girls' classes in the afternoons. Similarly, a pilot program to provide boarding facilities in girls' teacher training institutes met with resistance as parents preferred their daughters to live with relatives.

In the past, a major constraint in assigning female teachers to rural areas has been the lack of suitable housing. Morocco is providing teacher housing in new rural primary and lower secondary schools in two ongoing Bank projects with preference in assignment given to females and married couples. The link between female teachers and female enrollment in Morocco is being studied under current sector work.

Pakistan also provided female residences under an early Bank project, but this has not been successful as residences remained unoccupied. Women were reluctant to stay in residences provided at new rural primary schools because of social taboos and security risks. An added disincentive was that the housing allowance, representing up to 45 percent of the monthly salary, was automatically deducted if one chose to live in a residence.

On the other hand, Pakistan's experience with hiring locally-recruited female assistant teachers has proved to be a positive way to increase the number of female teachers in rural areas. In addition, female learning coordinators have been introduced to assist with supervision and on-the-job training for female teachers. There is evidence from an early project that the quality of instruction in project schools has improved due to a combination of increased supervision, in-service training by the learning coordinators, and the provision of instructional materials. Because of the past success of these measures, several ongoing Bank projects in Pakistan are pursuing this course. When a qualified local women is not available to staff a local girls' school, a less-qualified woman will be recruited and provided with in-service teacher training.

Similar measures are being introduced in the teacher training component of an ongoing Bank-assisted project in Bangladesh: improvements in facilities for women (lavatories and dormitories); gender-awareness in the curriculum; additional female faculty, whose salaries will be funded by the Bank; and modification of formal academic qualifications for entry to teacher training for girls in rural areas. According to current Government policy, 60 percent of primary teacher trainees must be women. The Gambia has also enacted a similar policy, whereby under a new Bank project, 40 percent of new primary teachers trainees must be women. In Pakistan, a new Bank-assisted project provides for special preference in enrollment for rural girls, in addition to scholarships and other financial and nonfinancial incentives, removal of age restrictions for entry/re-entry into teaching, and local recruitment and posting.

Sources: UNDP 1982; World Bank 1984b, 1986c, 1989d, 1989h, 1990f, 1990h, 1990i, 1990l, 1991b.

Box 4.9 Interventions to Overcome the Constraint of Opportunity Costs -- a Summary of Country Experience

Several measures have been adopted to reduce the time women and girls spend doing chores or to make it easier for girls to combine school and chores.

Flexible scheduling of school hours and the school calendar has been tried with favorable results in China and India. In 1979-80, a nonformal program offering night classes in 22 villages in Maharashtra State, India, addressed the problem of non-enrollment of working girls. The classes, aimed at dropouts and children who had never attended school, were held between 7 and 9 pm, 300 days a year. Local volunteers were recruited as instructors and the curriculum was geared to the community situation. Over a five-year period, more 4,000 children aged 9-14 enrolled, 75 percent of them female and all of them full-time workers engaged in household or farm work. The 25 percent dropout rate in project schools was much lower than the average 50-70 percent grade 1 drop out rate.

Similarly, in China's Kwangtung province in 1982, the Department of Education decided to run schools to suit local production needs. Full time schools operated only in the central village, and about 200 part-time and flexible classes were set up in surrounding villages. Female enrollments increased threefold over the previous year. In Yunan province, too, a system of 24 night schools and 29 morning and evening classes attracted mostly female students -- 70 percent compared with less than 50 percent of total enrollments before flexible schooling had been introduced. In fact, female enrollments in some village night schools exceeded 90 percent. Recent Bank-assisted projects in Bangladesh and Pakistan have introduced flexible scheduling of school hours and calendars, and the measure may be considered in Morocco.

Another measure is the provision of child care or permission to bring siblings to school. China has experimented with sibling care in several provinces where female enrollments lagged behind. In 1986, as part of an aggressive policy to promote Universal Primary Education in Gansu province, about 30 new village schools allowed girls to bring their younger siblings to class. This policy, along with other initiatives, succeeded in reaching the target of 3 percent growth in female primary enrollment in three years, and surpassed the target of 2 percent growth in female secondary enrollments. In the same province, worksite child-care centers for working mothers have improved girls' enrollments in urban areas. In Columbia,since 1987, the operation of community daycare programs for children under seven in poor neighborhoods has enabled many women and older girls to attend school or join the workforce. Under a current Bank-assisted project in Bangladesh, child-care facilities will be provided at new primary schools.

Improving the utility and type of education to make parents re-evaluate opportunity costs is another strategy. In some Bank projects, family life education (for example, basic principles of health, nutrition and child care) are included in the primary school curriculum, in such countries as the Gambia and Mali, to overcome parents' initial reluctance to enroll girls.

Among interventions that generally reduce women's work burden, one objective of labor saving technology is to free up girls' time for schooling. Examples are fuel-efficient woodburning stoves in Nepal, accessible water wells and simple mechanized grain mills in Burkina Faso, and dehullers and grinding mills to assist women and girls in The Gambia. Of course these measures may not work in the absence of other direct school interventions. For instance, an evaluation of the Burkina Faso program revealed that probably because schools were too distant, and the education content was unrelated to income generation, girls' enrollments did not increase despite the time saved.

Sources: Bellew and King 1991; Colletta and Sutton 1989; Naik 1987; UNESCO 1987; World Bank 1989a, 1989f, 1989h, 1990h, 1990i.

Improving Girls' Health and Nutrition

4.34 Children's health and nutritional status has consequences for school performance. Research in such diverse socioeconomic settings as Guatemala and Kenya has established that malnutrition inhibits children's learning even as early as the age of 2. A landmark nutrition study in Guatemala from 1967 to 1977 (which involved a recent resampling of the original participants) has shown that food supplements to children below 3 years of age are associated with higher enrollments, better school performance, and increased productivity even when the children grow up. The study was based on randomized feeding so that the impact of the food supplements could be measured net of other influences (INCAP research cited in Berg 1991a; Berg 1991b). The Bank's recent report on Sub-Saharan Africa: From Crisis to Sustainable Growth (1989) states that some of the high dropout and repetition rates in African schools "may be due to impaired mental abilities resulting from poor nutrition and micronutrient deficiencies" (p.80). Current research in Kenya is showing that four months of deworming medication has a significant effect on the cognitive powers of school children (Berg 1991a). Health and nutrition interventions are therefore likely to pay off in improved school attendance and performance and in a variety of other ways (Jamison and Leslie cited in Berg 1991a).

4.35 It is only common sense also to consider health and nutrition programs in school to help children survive and learn. Where sons are given strong preferential treatment, however, it may be difficult to improve girls' nutrition through school feeding programs, as parents may take food away from girls at home. Broader efforts to encourage parents to value the girl child and to improve the status of women may be needed. Bank operations in India as elsewhere are supporting nutrition programs for younger children and exploring possibilities for older children.

Instituting "Package Approaches": Lessons from Project Experience

4.36 What lessons can be learned from the changing character of the various components tried in these projects? First, education projects in very poor agrarian countries must have built-in components to address the direct costs and opportunity costs to parents of girls' education. For maximum impact on female enrollments, a simultaneous attack on several constraints seems most promising. This requires careful analysis beforehand of constraints, identification of effective combinations of measures to overcome them, monitoring and mid-course corrections as measures are tried, and an evaluation of their impact. No single package of "key elements" applies in all countries -- but in a given country, a "minimum combination" may be needed to achieve much impact. The experience of several countries -- including China, Korea, and Sri Lanka (discussed earlier) -- suggests that a package approach does work. By and large, early Bank-assisted projects implemented single interventions and thus did not address the multiple constraints affecting girls. Consequently, the results were disappointing in most cases (see Appendix table 1). By contrast, projects that implemented package approaches had better results. Of particular interest is the Bangladesh Fourth Primary project (1980-86) which addressed both household-level and school-level constraints by combining a variety of program actions such as improved school facilities, female teachers, reduced costs (free textbooks), and special incentives (scholarships). As a result, female enrollments improved 9 percent annually in project areas compared with only 2 percent in the country as a whole. In countries where direct costs are high for very poor families, subsidies are necessary, but targeting is equally important. Where poverty is regionally concentrated, targeting geographically disadvantaged areas is a promising approach.

4.37 Second, increase the number and proportion of female teachers. Teacher recruitment and training initiatives especially for women have generally been helpful, although evidence about boarding schools attracting more women for training has been mixed -- this was successful in Syria but not in Yemen (see Appendix table 2). The reason for failure in some instances appears to be cultural insensitivity in the project design.

4.38 Third, involve the community. The role of the community in Guatemala's primary scholarship program for girls was instrumental in identifying the "right" project beneficiaries and overseeing the project's implementation. Bangladesh's "satellite" schools were popular partly because schools were closer and partly because the community chose the operating hours so that the schedules did not interfere with the work rural children were expected to do. In China, India, Morocco, Nepal, and Papua New Guinea, community input -- from awareness campaigns to educate the community to active community management of the project -- has been key to the success of various programs designed to raise female enrollments. These efforts underscore the need for project designs to be responsive to the people's cultural sensitivities.

4.39 Fourth, address the financial implications of measures to increase female enrollment. Raising girls' enrollments will require some special additional costs in many countries and little information is available on what these costs may be. Logic does permit characterizing the costs to some degree. Constructing and equipping new schools and providing teachers for them will obviously cost money -- but the question is what the additional cost would be to make them more responsive to the specific needs of girls. Opting for many small schools instead of a few larger centralized schools does not obviously cost more -- communities may be more willing to contribute to the former, and they may be easier and less expensive to build. Adding the necessary lavatories or otherwise ensuring girls' privacy is unlikely to cost much, especially if parents are consulted about how this could be achieved. There may be some additional administrative costs associated with the decentralization, but even that is not obvious -- and the demonstrated increased effectiveness of such schools may more than compensate for the additional costs, producing more cost-effective education. Building new girls' schools could be expensive if no construction is planned, but allocating some planned schools to girls may not be, as long as population densities are heavy enough so that at least two schools would have been built fairly close by. Similarly it may be possible to shift children among existing schools to create some single-sex schools.

4.40 Revamping textbooks to remove gender bias is costly if textbooks are not due for replacement, but not if they are to be revised anyway. Improving the relevance of curriculum so that both boys and girls learn the essentials of verbal and mathematical skills may entail some costs, but what is the value of irrelevant education? Certainly the additional cost of making curriculum relevant for girls should be modest, perhaps including more information on tasks that most women must or choose to undertake. Awareness campaigns and efforts to involve parents and the broader community are also not likely to cost much -- and may well pay dividends in improved attendance and learning. Thus, in many circumstances, it is reasonable to think that a good deal can be tried at relatively modest cost -- and possibly with gains in cost-effectiveness.

4.41 The question is whether these low-cost possibilities are enough to make a difference -- does the "package" have to include measures to cut costs to parents, such as scholarships? The evidence is not conclusive but does suggest that in circumstances where girls' enrollments are very low and considerably lower than boys', some such steps may be needed. Waiving or reducing fees for all children differentially helps girls because imposing fees differentially hurts girls more in some countries: special scholarships or incentives for girls will probably be needed to make real gains in female enrollment in the near term. Whether this is considered "affordable" depends on what value the government and the broader society place on the social benefits of female education: the Government of Bangladesh, for example, has decided the value exceeds the cost. Of course, the additional costs involved even in scholarships to increase female enrollment are likely to be negligible compared to present military expenditures in many countries. Still, the costs must be covered, and for governments facing severe budgetary pressures, this will pose a considerable challenge.

Box 4.10 Package Approaches to Overcome the Constraints for Girls: Examples from Recent Bank-Assisted Projects

Experience indicates that where constraints on female access are pervasive and severe, multiple interventions are needed to raise girls' enrollments. Many new and ongoing Bank-assisted projects contain multiple interventions. Although they are too recent to evaluate, they suggest the potential of the "package approach."

Bangladesh's General Education Project (1990): This project addresses the binding constraints of direct and opportunity costs in a poor agrarian economy. A pilot program aims to build 200 satellite schools in underserved/underenrolled areas closer to girls' homes. The satellite schools, grades 1-3, will be staffed by locally recruited female teachers but linked to larger central schools. A new feature will be provision of child care for younger siblings at the schools. The Female Education Scholarship Program for secondary school girls, which decreased dropouts from 14.7 percent in the program's first year to 3.5 percent in 1987 and raised the attendance of even non-scholarship girls, will be continued. Experimental programs to make government schools more attractive to girls include school feeding, provision of uniforms, and community outreach programs. More female teachers will be hired and their salaries will be financed by the Bank on a declining basis. Revised selection criteria to recruit women at a 60/40 ratio over men and active recruitment of women are expected to raise the percentage of female primary school teachers from 19 to 50 percent of the teaching force over the next decade. The project also provides improved teacher training facilities for women and aims to reduce gender bias in teaching methods and attitudes. Gender stereotypes will also be removed from textbooks and other teaching materials, and the primary curriculum will be revised to improve the relevance of school for girls. Continuous supervision and monitoring will provide for more frequent evaluations, particularly of the measures for girls.

The Gambia's Education Sector Project (1990): Expanded coverage of primary schools in rural areas and the lowering of the school entry age from 8 to 6 years are expected to raise girls' enrollments considerably. Only 33 percent of primary school teachers are women and less than half are considered qualified. Modified admission criteria for teacher training will help to recruit at least 40 percent female candidates by 1996-97, and an in-service teacher training program will provide upgrading with salary increases to graduates. Teacher training will include programs aimed at eliminating sex-role stereotyping in the classroom. Positive female role models and family life education will be written into the primary curriculum. At the secondary level, new science and mathematics clubs for girls will award fellowships, awards, and internships for girls who perform well. Monitoring is built in to assess the impact of the various measures.

Morocco's Rural Basic Education Project (1991) aims to increase participation in upper basic education (grades 6-9) in rural areas, particularly of girls, by addressing distance and financial and cultural constraints. In 1989/90, girls represented only 22 percent of rural middle school enrollment compared with 41 percent nationally. The construction of 250 new middle schools close to targeted communities is designed to counter the weak demand for primary education in rural areas. All schools will have canteens, and scholarships will be provided for meals. Thirty of the new schools will have boarding facilities and will provide boarding scholarships. In 1989/90, girls accounted for fewer than 10 percent of boarders in rural middle schools and fewer than 20 percent in middle schools nationwide. Half of the scholarships and boarding places will be for girls, a measure expected to provide strong incentives for parents to enroll their daughters in middle school. Another measure to defray school costs is a program of low-cost textbooks for all students. Monitoring of these interventions will ascertain the impact on school access and participation in rural areas, especially of girls.

The Pakistan Sindh Education Project (1990): New schools will be built where there is no school available within 2.5 km. for boys and 1.5 km. for girls and where the population in the catchment area exceeds 100. Moreover, the new girls' and mixed schools will be provided with toilets, water supply, and boundary walls. To insure greater attendance, a more appropriate school calendar will be introduced, along with prizes and incentives for teachers who develop measures to encourage parents to send and retain girls at school. In addition to addressing school-level constraints, household level constraints have been addressed by providing free textbooks for rural primary girls, scholarships for rural secondary girls, and a pilot program to abolish uniform requirements in rural areas. Other pilot programs include school feeding with local community management, automatic promotion in grades 1-3, and flexible school hours in 150 rural schools. To attract more females to teaching, age requirements have been amended and local recruitment and posting will be practiced. Where shortages persist, the entrance qualification for female teachers will be lowered. The project aims to increase rural primary girls' enrollment rates from the current 14% to 23 percent in 1995. Monitoring and evaluation will assess the effectiveness of pilot initiatives in project areas.

The above projects are in various stages of implementation. To know the results of these ongoing experiments, it is important to collect baseline data with appropriate control groups built into sample design.

Sources: World Bank 1990h, 1990i, 1990l, 1991b.

4.42 Rationalizing expenditures within the education sector may free up some resources: in many countries universities are very highly subsidized even though the social returns are greater at the primary and secondary levels and relatively few poorer students attend universities. But imposing user fees in universities is politically difficult. So careful targeting and monitoring of programs to subsidize female education -- or any education -- are obviously needed. Means tests are also notoriously difficult to establish and enforce, but some regional targeting may be possible where the incidence of poverty varies geographically in a fairly regular way. Community participation in the design and administration of programs evidently helps to overcome political difficulties and ensure that resources are used as intended. (Community participation in the targeting of recipients and supervision of payments was instrumental in the success of Guatemala's primary scholarship program for girls.) Moreover, experience in health, family planning, and nutrition programs certainly demonstrates that community participation can improve public understanding of targeting issues and the cost-effectiveness of programs (see, for example, World Bank 1986d).

4.43 Finally, and as a priority, monitoring and research should be undertaken to establish the costs and impacts of different efforts (and different combinations of efforts) to improve girls' education, particularly in the context of Bank-financed projects where innovative approaches are being tried. To be done properly, this will require sample surveys at the household level disaggregated by gender and community-level information to sort out the relative importance of different influences on girls' schooling. The sample surveys must be done before the project begins to provide a baseline view of project areas and control groups. The surveys should then be repeated after the project has been underway long enough to have an effect. In the interim, monitoring and mid-course corrections should be undertaken and enough data collected to show what was done and why. Monitoring should track male and female enrollments as a minimum and if possible also cover students' performance, the main educational inputs, and other potentially important influences on childrens' education such as changes in income for fathers or mothers. Some recent Bank-assisted projects provide for baseline data. A few also provide for periodic data collection to show the effectiveness of various interventions (see Appendix table 2). But, monitoring and evaluation have rarely exceeded 2 percent of project costs. The need to generate information for testing alternatives may necessitate higher than normal allocations to this activity in project budgets. This should be regarded as a necessary investment to gain knowledge on what works. Only this kind of research can establish firmly what works to let girls learn.

World Bank Investment in Improving Female Enrollments

Overall Progress

4.44 Over 1972-80, 105 out of 153 Bank-assisted education projects addressed primary and secondary enrollments, many in Africa and Latin America (LAC) (see table 4.2). Of these, 20 projects (19 percent) acknowledged the presence of one or more gender issues, and about half as many contained specific programs of action to improve female education. The regional breakdown shows less attention to female education in Latin America, but this region had already achieved a high degree of gender parity by 1970. Despite the pervasive lack of parity in Africa, Asia, and Middle Eastern (EMENA) countries, relatively little was done to recognize or deal with the problem there.[1]

[1] LAC refers to Latin America and the Caribbean. EMENA refers to the World Bank regional classification of Europe, Middle East and North Africa.

Table 4.2: Review of Bank-Assisted Education Projects

	1972–1980					1981–1991*				
	Africa	Asia	EMENA	LAC	Total	Africa	Asia	EMENA	LAC	Total
1. All Education Projects**	55	33	36	29	153	60	60	42	30	192
2. Education projects with primary/secondary components (including teacher training)	46	14	22	23	105	52	24	23	16	115
3. Those acknowledging gender issues										
(a) Number of projects	7	3	7	3	20	28	11	13	5	57
(b) Total investment (Millions of US$)***	134.5	51.4	111.6	54.6	357.1	636.5	379.4	515.9	110.6	1642.4
4. Projects with significant action to address gender problem										
(a) Number of projects	2	3	5	0	10	11	6	11	0	28
(b) Total investment (Millions of US$)***	41.8	51.4	77.8	0	171	312.3	214	449.9	0	966.1
5. Row 4 as a % of row 3										
(a) Number of projects	28.6%	100.0%	71.4%	0.0%	50.0%	39.3%	54.5%	84.6%	0.0%	49.1%
(b) Total investment (Millions of US$)***	31.1%	100.0%	69.7%	0.0%	47.9%	49.1%	56.4%	87.2%	0.0%	58.8%
6. % change in projects with significant action to address gender problem (1981–91 over 1972–80)										
(a) Number of projects						550.0%	200.0%	220.0%	0.0%	280.0%
(b) Total investment (Millions of US$)***						747.1%	416.3%	578.3%	0.0%	565.0%

Sources: World Bank Staff Appraisal Reports.

Notes: *cut-off date January 31, 1991; **Approved by the Board; ***Expressed in 1980 dollars

4.45 During the 1980s the situation improved. More Bank-financed education projects recognized gender issues and included specific actions to redress inequities. Nearly half of all projects in Africa, Asia, and the Middle East acknowledged gender issues; half of these projects in Africa and Asia, and about three-fourths in the Middle East, included specific actions. A slightly higher proportion of projects in Latin America countries did acknowledge gender issue in the 1980s, but none had any specific program of action. Details of recent and ongoing Bank-assisted projects with interventions to improve female enrollments are given in Appendix table 1. On the whole, attention to gender increased substantially in the 1980s over 1972-80.

4.46 As shown in chapter 2, a substantial body of research (including in-house research in the Bank) conducted in the 1970s established that the social returns on primary and secondary schooling were higher than those on tertiary education, especially for girls. This finding had an effect on Bank lending to education. Between 1972 and 1980, 69 percent of all projects addressed primary and secondary enrollments; the rest addressed higher and vocational education. But in the 1980s this ratio dropped to 60 percent. Female participation rates are still generally higher in primary and secondary schools than at the tertiary level, so this shift is not in the interests of gender equity.

Conclusions

4.47 Country-level project experience on what works to improve female enrollments is too recent to draw firm conclusions. Several ongoing projects are now testing various approaches. Nonetheless, some patterns emerge. Many projects were more successful at providing more appealing types of schooling than in addressing household or labor market constraints on demand for female schooling. Improving access to schools and enhancing their quality and cultural suitability did promote female enrollments -- but mainly where the direct and opportunity costs to the family of sending girls to school were not overwhelming. Where these costs pose a heavy burden to parents, it appears that they must be eased to increase female enrollments sharply. Future projects need to take an integrated view of the various constraints, especially the direct and opportunity costs, and include a package of remedies in the project design. That such initiatives are possible is demonstrated by recent projects in Bangladesh and Morocco.

4.48 Incentives to overcome direct and opportunity costs involve subsidizing school inputs and providing scholarships -- these may be essential and justifiable on economic and social grounds. But they may also increase project costs, and they can be misdirected. Appropriate targeting and management are crucial if education budgets are to be used effectively and kept affordable.

4.49 The Bank's efforts to address female education are evolving and improving. In the initial years, they addressed only one or two school-level constraints. More projects in recent years have begun to address several constraints at once. These projects should be used to rigorously test alternative strategies for increasing female enrollments (collecting baseline data and assessing results). Research needs to be directed toward establishing the cost-effectiveness of alternative strategies in varying country situations reflecting current economics as well as social conditions. Such a blending of innovative operations and research ought to be a priority in all programs to develop human resources, not just to let girls learn.

REFERENCES

Abadzi, H. I. Patel and M. Schifferaw. 1991. "Nonformal Education and Training Programs." In King, E. and M.A. Hill. 1991. Women's Education in Developing Countries. Washington, D.C.: World Bank.

Acharya, M. and L. Bennett. 1981. The Status of Women in Nepal, vol. II, Field Studies: Rural Women of Nepal, An Aggregate Analysis and Summary of Eight Village Studies. Centre for Economic Development and Administration. Kathmandu: Tribhuvan University.

Alderman, H. and S. Chisti. 1989. "Simultaneous Determination of Household and Market-Oriented Activities of Women in Rural Pakistan." Paper presented for Conference on Family, Gender Differences, and Development, Yale University, September 4-6, 1989.

Alderman, H. and V. Kozel. 1989. "Formal and Informal Sector Wage Determination in Urban Low-Income Neighborhoods in Pakistan." LSMS Working Paper No. 65. Washington, D.C.: World Bank.

Armitage, J., J. Neto, R. Harbison, D. Holsinger and R. Leite. 1986. "School Quality and Achievement in Rural Brazil." Education and Training Series Discussion Paper 25. Washington, D.C.: World Bank.

Barnes, C. and L. Warner. 1982. "Kenyan Smallholdings and the Division of Labour." Mimeo.

Baxter, M. 1986. "New Development in Agricultural Extension." Washington, D.C.: World Bank.

Becker, G. 1967. "Human Capital and the Personal Distribution of Income: An Analytical Approach." Ann Arbor: University of Michigan, Woytinsky Lecture, republished in G. Becker, Human Capital. Second edition, 1975, 94-117. New York: NBER.

Beenstock, M. and P. Sturdy. 1990. "Determinants of Infant Mortality in Regional India." World Development 18:443-53 (March).

Begum, K., S. Akhter and S. Rahman. 1988. "An Evaluation of BRAC's Primary Education Programme." In Bellew, R. and E. King. 1991. "Promoting Girls' and Women's Education: Lessons from the Past." PHREE Working Paper No. 715. Washington, D.C.: World Bank.

Behrman, J. 1990. "Women's Schooling and Nonmarket Productivity: A Survey and a Reappraisal." PHRWD Working Paper. Washington, D.C.: World Bank.

Behrman, J. 1991. "Investing in Female Education for Development: Women in Development Strategy for the 1990s in Asia and the Near East." Mimeo. Philadelphia: University of Pennsylvania.

Behrman, J. and C. Sussangkarn. 1989. "Parental Schooling and Child Outcomes: Mother Versus Father, Schooling Quality, and Interactions." Mimeo, Philadelphia: University of Pennsylvania.

Bellew, R. and E. King. 1991. "Promoting Girls' and Women's Education: Lessons from the Past." PHREE Working Paper No. 715. Washington, D.C.: World Bank.

Berg, A. 1991b. "Sliding Toward Nutrition Malpractice -- Time to Reconsider and Redeploy." Martin Forman Memorial Lecture, Hyatt Regency Hotel, Crystal City, June 24, 1991.

Birdsall, N. 1980. "A Cost of Siblings: Child Schooling in Urban Colombia." Research in Population Economics, 2, 115-150.

-----. 1985. "Public Inputs and Child Schooling in Brazil." Journal of Development Economics 18:1 (May-June), 67-86.

Bustillo, I. 1989. "Female Educational Attainment in Latin America." PHREE Background Paper Series 16. Washington, D.C.: World Bank.

Callaway, B.J. 1984. "Ambiguous Consequences of the Socialisation and Seclusion of Hausa Women." in Hyde, K. 1989. "Improving Women's Education in Sub-Saharan Africa: A Review of the Literature. PHREE Background Paper Series 15. Washington, D.C.: World Bank.

Cain, M. 1977. "The Economic Activities of Children in a Village in Bangladesh." Population and Development Review 3, 201-227.

Chernikovsky, D. 1985. "Socio-economic and Demographic Aspects of School Enrollment and Attendance in Rural Botswana." Economic Development and Cultural Change 33: 319-32.

Cochrane, S. 1979. "Education and Fertility: What Do We Really Know?" World Bank Staff Occasional Paper No. 26. Washington, D.C.

Cochrane, S., O'Hara, D. and J. Leslie. 1980. "The Effects of Education on Health." World Bank Staff Working Papers, No. 405. Washington, D.C.: World Bank.

-----. 1982. "Parental Education and Child Health: Intracountry Evidence." Health Policy and Education, 2. (March), 213-250.

Colletta, N. and M. Sutton. 1989. "Achieving and Sustaining Universal Primary Education: International Experience Relevant to India." PHR Working Paper Series 166. Washington, D.C.: World Bank.

Collier et al. 1991a. "Gender Differences in Access to Schooling in the Cote d'Ivoire." Draft. PHRWD Division. World Bank.

Collier et al. 1991b. "Gender Differences in Access to Secondary Schooling in Rural Kenya." Draft. PHRWD Division. World Bank.

Cooksey, B. and Ishumi, A. 1986. "A Critical Review of Policy and Practice in Tanzania Secondary Education Since 1967." Department of Eduction, University of Dar es Salaam, Tanzania.

Creative Associates. 1990. "Girls' Scholarships: A Comparative Review." Draft. Mimeo. Washington, D.C.

Csapo, M. 1981. "Religious, Social and Economic Factors Hindering the Education of Girls in Northern Nigeria." Comparative Education 17:3, 311-319.

Davison, J. and M. Kanyuka. 1990. "An Ethnographic Study of Factors that Affect the Education of Girls in Southern Malawi." In S. Grant-Lewis and others 1990. "Constraints to Girls' Persistence in Primary School and Women's Employment Opportunities in the Education Service." A Report to the Ministry of Education and Culture and USAID Malawi. Lilongwe.

Demographic and Health Surveys. 1990a. Newsletter, Vol. 3, No. 2. Summer.

Demographic and Health Surveys. 1990b. "Women's Education -- Findings from Demographic and Health Surveys." Paper prepared for the World Conference on Education for All, Bangkok, Thailand, March 1990.

DeTray, D. 1988. "Government Policy, Household Behavior and the Distribution of Schooling: A Case Study of Malaysia." In T.P. Schultz, ed., 1988, Research in Population Economics: A Research Annual, Vol. 6, 303-36. Greenwich, CT: JAI Press.

Dixon-Muller, R. and R. Anker. 1988. "Assessing Women's Economic Contributions to Development". Background Papers for Training in Population, Human Resources and Development Planning, Paper No. 6. Geneva: ILO.

Duraiswamy, P. 1989. "Fertility and Child Schooling in Rural India: Evidence from Aggregate Panel Data." Paper presented at a conference on the family, gender differences, and development at the Economic Growth Center, Yale University, September 4-6, 1989.

El Sanabary, N. 1989. "Determinants of Women's Eduction in the Middle East and North Africa: Illustrations from Seven Countries." PHREE Background Paper Series. Washington, D.C.: World Bank.

Eshiwani, G.S. 1985. The Education of Women in Kenya: 1975-1984, Bureau of Educational Research, Kenyatta University College, Nairobi. In World Bank. 1989. Kenya: The Role of Women in Economic Development. Washington, D.C.

Evenson, R., B. Popkin and E. Quizon. 1980. "Nutrition, Work and Demographic Behavior in Rural Philippine Households" in H. Binswanger and others, eds. 1980. Rural Household Studies in Asia. Singapore: Singapore University Press.

Government of Balochistan. 1991. "Human Resource Survey: Teacher Supply and Distribution." Interim Report for Semi-Urban Villages." Draft. Balochistan: Office of Additional Director Primary Education. Education Department Quetta. Pakistan.

Government of India. 1990. The Lesser Child. In United Nations. 1990. SCN News, No. 6.

Grisay, A. 1984. "Analyse des Inégalities de Rendement Liées au Sexe de l'Elève dans l'Enseignement Primaire Ivoirien." International Review of Education XXX, 25-39.

Hanushek, E. and R. Harbison. Forthcoming. "Investments in School Quality: Evidence from Brazil." Paper presented at a conference on family, gender differences, and development at the Economic Growth Center, Yale University, September 4-6, 1989.

Herz, B. and S. Khandker, eds. 1991. "Women's Work, Education and Family Welfare in Peru." World Bank Discussion Paper 116. Washington, D.C.: World Bank.

Holt, S. and H. Ribe. 1991. "Developing Financial Institutions for the Poor and Reducing Barriers to Access for Women." World Bank Discussion Paper 117. Washington, D.C.: World Bank.

Hyde, K. 1989. "Improving Women's Education in Sub-Saharan Africa: A Review of the Literature. PHREE Background Paper Series 15. Washington, D.C.: World Bank.

ILO. 1989. Technical Background Paper for the Meeting of Experts on Special Protective Measures for Women and Equality of Opportunity and Treatment. Geneva, 10-17 October. MEPMW/1989/1.

INCAP research cited in Berg, A. 1991a. New and Noteworthy in Nutrition, No. 12, February 5. World Bank. PHRHN Division. Mimeo.

Jamison, D. and J. Leslie cited in Berg, A. 1990. New and Noteworthy in Nutrition, No. 9, May 3. World Bank, PHRHN Division. Mimeo.

Jamison, D. and M. Lockheed. 1987. "Participation in Schooling: Determinants and Learning Outcomes in Nepal." Economic Development and Cultural Change, 279-306.

Jimenez, E. and M. Lockheed. 1989. "Enhancing Girls' Learning Through Single-Sex Education: Evidence and a Policy Conundrum." Educational Evaluation and Policy Analysis, Vol. 11, No. 2. pp. 117-142.

Khandker, S. 1990. "Labor Market Participation, Returns to Education and Male-Female Wage Differences in Peru." PRE Working Paper 461. Washington, D.C.: World Bank.

Khandker, S. 1991. "Earnings, Occupational Choice and Mobility in Segmented Labor Markets of India." Washington, D.C.: World Bank.

Kelly, G. and C. Elliott, eds. 1982. Women's Education in the Third World: Comparative Perspectives. Albany, NY: State University of New York Press.

King, E. and R. Bellew. 1988. "Education Policy and Schooling Levels in Peru." Mimeo. Washington, D.C.: World Bank.

King, E. and R. Bellew. 1991. "Gains in the Education of Peruvian Women, 1940-1980" in Herz, B. and S. Khandker, eds. 1991. "Women's Work, Education and Family Welfare in Peru". World Bank Discussion Paper 116. Washington, D.C.: World Bank.

King, E. and A. Hill. forthcoming. Women's Education in Developing Countries: A Review of Barriers, Benefits and Policy. Washington, D.C.: World Bank.

King, E. and L. Lillard. 1983. Determinants of Schooling Attainment and Enrollment Rates in the Philippines. Santa Monica, CA: The Rand Corporation.

-----. 1987. "Education Policy and Schooling Attainment in Malaysia and the Philippines." Economics of Education Review 6:2 (November), 167-181.

Kozel, V. and H. Alderman. 1988. "Factors Determining Work Participation and Labor Supply Decisions in Pakistan's Urban Areas." Paper prepared for the fifth annual meeting of Pakistan Society for Development Economics. Washington, D.C.: International Food Policy Research Institute.

Lavy, V. Forthcoming. "Supply Constraints and Investment in Human Capital: Schooling in Rural Ghana." Washington, D.C.: World Bank.

Lee, V. and M. Lockheed. 1990. "The Effects of Single-Sex Schooling on Achievement and Attitudes in Nigeria." Comparative Education Review, Vol. 34, No. 2.

Lockheed, M., A. Verspoor et al. 1991. Improving Primary Education in Developing Countries. Washington, D.C.: World Bank.

Malathy, R. 1989. "Labor Supply Behaviour of Married Women in Urban India." Paper presented at a conference on the family, gender differences, and development at the Economic Growth Center, Yale University, September 4-6, 1989.

Mensch, B. H. Lentzner and S. Preston. 1986. Socio-Economic Differentials in Child Mortality in Developing Countries. New York: United Nations.

Moock, P. 1973. "Managerial Ability in Small-Farm Production: An Analysis of Maize Yields in the Vihiga Division of Kenya." Ph.D. dissertation in Economics. Columbia University, New York.

Naik, C. 1987. "Educating Rural Girls: A Review of an Action-Research Project." International Review of Education 33, 495-511.

Nkinyangi, J. 1982. "Access to Primary Education in Kenya: The Contradictions of Public Policy." Comparative Education Review 26:2, 199-217.

Pitt, M. and M. Rosenzweig. 1989. "Estimating the Intrafamily Incidence of Illness: Child Health and Gender Inequality in the Allocation of Time in Indonesia." Paper presented at a conference on the Family, Gender Differences, and Development, Yale University, September 4-6, 1989.

Psacharopoulos, G. and Z. Tzannatos, eds. Forthcoming. "Female Employment and Pay in Latin America: A Regional Study." Human Resources Division, Technical Department, Latin America and Caribbean Region, World Bank.

Robertson, C., and I. Berger, eds. 1986 Women and Class in Africa in Hyde, K. 1989. "Improving Women's Education in Sub-Saharan Africa: A Review of the Literature." PHREE Background Paper Series 15. Washington, D.C.: World Bank.

Robinson, W., N. Makary and A. Rugh. 1987. "Fourth Annual Report of the Study of USAID Contributions to the Egyptian Basic Education Program." Washington, D.C. Office of Women in Development, U.S. Agency for International Development.

Rosenzweig, M. 1980. "Household and Non-household Activities of Youths: Issues of Modeling, Data and Estimation Strategies." ILO Working Paper No. 90. Geneva.

Rosenzweig, M. and T.P. Schultz. 1982. "Market Opportunities, Genetic Endowments and the Intrafamily Distribution: Child Survival in Rural India." American Economic Review, 72 (September), 803-815.

Saito, K. and C. Weidemann. 1990. "Agricultural Extension for Women Farmers in Africa." World Bank Discussion Papers, No. 103. Washington, D.C.: World Bank.

Saito, K. and D. Spurling. 1991. "Agricultural Extension and Research for Women Farmers." Washington, D.C.: World Bank.

Sajogyo, P. and others. 1980. Different Perspectives, West Java, Project on Rural Household Economics and the Role of Women, in FAO 1985, Women in Developing Agriculture, Rome.

Sambamoorthi, V. 1984. "Labor Market Discrimination Against Women in India." Working Paper No. 58. Women in Development, East Lansing: Michigan State University.

Schultz, T.P. 1989a. "Returns to Women's Education." PHRWD Working Paper No. 001. Washington, D.C.: World Bank.

-----. 1989b. "Women in Development: Objectives, Frameworks and Policy Interventions." PHRWD Working Paper No. 200. Washington, D.C.: World Bank.

Searle, B. 1989. Personal communication.

Sen, A. 1987. "Notes for the Seminar on 'Women's Issues in Development Policy' at the International Center for Research on Women on 27 March 1987." Mimeo.

Stromquist, N. 1987. "School-Related Determinants of Female Primary School Participation and Achievement in Developing Countries: An Annotated Bibliography." World Bank Discussion Paper No. 83. Washington, D.C.

Thomas, D. 1989. "Intra-Household Resource Allocation: An Inferential Approach." Paper presented at a conference on the family, gender differences, and development at the Economic Growth Center, Yale University, September 4-6, 1989.

Thomas, D. 1990. "Like Father, Like Son: Gender Differences in Household Resource Allocations." LSMS Working Paper, No. 79. Washington, D.C.: World Bank.

Thomas, D. J. Strauss and M. H. Henriques. 1990. "Child Survival, Height for Age and Household Characteristics in Brazil." Journal of Development Economics.

Tilak, J. 1987. The Economics of Inequality in Education. New Delhi: Sage Publications.

Tilak, J. 1989. "Female Schooling in East Asia." PHREE Background Paper Series. Washington, D.C.: World Bank.

UNDP. 1982. "Nepal: Teacher Training (Equal Access of Women to Education) -- Project Findings and Recommendations." Paris.

UNESCO. 1979. Statistical Yearbook.

UNESCO. 1984a. Towards Universalization of Primary Education in Asia and the Pacific: Korea. Bangkok.

UNESCO. 1984b. Towards Universalization of Primary Education in Asia and the Pacific: Sri Lanka. Bangkok.

UNESCO. 1984c. The Dropout Problem in Primary Education: Towards Universalization of Primary Education in Asia and the Pacific -- Some Case Studies. Regional Office for Education in Asia and the Pacific. Bangkok.

UNESCO. 1987a. Universal Primary Education for Girls -- China. Principle Regional Office for Asia and the Pacific. Bangkok.

UNESCO. 1987b. Universal Primary Education for Girls -- Papua New Guinea. Principle Regional Office for Asia and the Pacific. Bangkok.

UNESCO. 1990. Statistical Yearbook.

UNICEF. 1987. Situation Analysis of Children and Women in Pakistan. Government of Pakistan and and UNICEF Country Programme of Cooperation 1988-1992. Islamabad.

Wolfe, B. and J. Behrman. 1984. "Determinants of Women's Health Status and Healthcare Utilization in a Developing Country: A Latent Variable Approach." Review of Economics and Statistics 56:4 (November), 696-703.

Winter, C. 1991. Personal Communication.

World Bank. 1972. "Staff Appraisal Report Jordan First Education Project." Rpt. No. PE-36a. Washington, D.C.

World Bank. 1975a. "Staff Appraisal Report Malawi Second Education Project." Rpt. No. 877-MAI. Washington, D.C.

World Bank. 1975b. "Staff Appraisal Report Yemen Arab Republic Second Education Project." Rpt. No. 790-YAR. Washington, D.C.

World Bank. 1976. "Staff Appraisal Report Papua New Guinea First Education Project." Rpt. No. 1210-PNG. Washington, D.C.

World Bank. 1977. "Staff Appraisal Report Syria First Education Project." Rpt. No. 1513-SYR. Washington, D.C.

World Bank. 1979a. "Project Performance Audit Report Jordan First Education Project (Cr. 285-JO)." Rpt. No. 2494. Washington, D.C.

World Bank. 1979b. "Staff Appraisal Report Pakistan Primary Education Project." Rpt. No. 2305 -PAK. Washington, D.C.

World Bank. 1980a. "Staff Appraisal Report Bangladesh Fourth Education Project (Primary Education)." Rpt. No. 2964-BD. Washington, D.C.

World Bank. 1980b. "Staff Appraisal Report Papua New Guinea Primary Education Project." Rpt. No. 3027b-PNG. Washington, D.C.

World Bank. 1980c. "Staff Appraisal Report Tanzania Seventh Education Project." Rpt. No. 2782-TA. Washington, D.C.

World Bank. 1980d. World Development Report. Washington, D.C.

World Bank. 1981. "Staff Appraisal Report Malawi Fourth Education Project." Rpt. No. 3183-MAI. Washington, D.C.

World Bank. 1983a. "Project Completion Report Malawi Second Education Project (Cr. 590-MLI). "Rpt. No. 4572. Washington, D.C.

World Bank. 1983b. "Staff Appraisal Report Jordan Sixth Education Project." Rpt. No. 4685-JO. Washington, D.C.

World Bank. 1983c. "Staff Appraisal Report Yemen Arab Republic Fifth Education Project." Rpt. No. 4223-YAR. Washington, D.C.

World Bank. 1984a. "Project Performance Audit Report Papua New Guinea First Education Project (Cr. 661-PNG)." Rpt. No. 5126. Washington, D.C.

World Bank. 1984b. "Project Performance Audit Report Yemen Arab Republic Second Education Project (Cr. 611-YAR)." Rpt. No. 5086. Washington, D.C.

World Bank. 1984c. "Staff Appraisal Report Djibouti First Education Project." Rpt. No. 5215-DJI. Washington, D.C.

World Bank. 1984d. "Staff Appraisal Report Oman Second Education Project." Rpt. No. 4958-OM. Washington, D.C.

World Bank. 1984e. "Staff Appraisal Report Yemen Arab Republic Sixth Education Project." Rpt. No. 4634-YAR. Washington, D.C.

World Bank. 1984f. World Development Report. Washington, D.C.

World Bank. 1985a. "Project Performance Audit Report Syria First Education Project (Ln. 1480)." Rpt. No. 5640. Washington, D.C.

World Bank. 1985b. "Staff Appraisal Report Bangladesh Second Primary Education Project." Rpt. No. 5362-BD. Washington, D.C.

World Bank. 1985c. "Staff Appraisal Report Pakistan Second Primary Education Project." Rpt. No. 5363-PAK. Washington, D.C.

World Bank. 1986a. Population, Growth and Policies in Sub-Saharan Africa. Washington, D.C.

World Bank. 1986b. " Staff Appraisal Report Solomon Islands Secondary Education Project." Rpt. No. 5645-SOL. Washington, D.C.

World Bank. 1986c. " Staff Appraisal Report Morocco Education Sector Reform Program." Rpt. No. 5923-MOR. Washington, D.C.

World Bank. 1986d. World Development Report. Washington, D.C.

World Bank. 1987a. "Staff Appraisal Report Ethiopia Seventh Education Project." Rpt. No. 6931-ET. Washington, D.C.

World Bank 1987b. "Staff Appraisal Report Malawi Education Sector Credit." Rpt. No. 6428-MAI. Washington, D.C.

World Bank. 1987c. "Staff Appraisal Report Oman Third Education Project." Rpt. No. 6584-OM. Washington, D.C.

World Bank. 1987d. "Staff Appraisal Report Pakistan Third Primary Education Project." Rpt. No. 6492-PAK. Washington, D.C.

World Bank. 1987e. "Staff Appraisal Report Yemen Arab Republic Teacher Training Project." Rpt. No. 6463-YAR. Washington, D.C.

World Bank. 1988a. "Staff Appraisal Report Bhutan Primary Education Project." Rpt. No. 7010-BHU. Washington, D.C.

World Bank. 1988b. "Staff Appraisal Report China Teacher Training Project." Rpt. No. 7189-CHA. Washington, D.C.

World Bank. 1988c. "Staff Appraisal Report Maldives Education and Training Project." Rpt. No. 7367-MAL. Washington, D.C.

World Bank. 1988d. "Staff Appraisal Report Mauritania Education Sector Restructuring Project." Rpt. No. 7213-MAU. Washington, D.C.

World Bank. 1989a. "Gambia Women in Development Country Assessment." Draft. AF5PH. Mimeo.

World Bank. 1989b. Kenya: The Role of Women in Economic Development. World Bank Country Study. Washington, D.C.

World Bank. 1989c. Sub-Saharan Africa: From Crisis to Sustainable Growth. Washington, D.C.

World Bank. 1989d. "Yemen Arab Republic: Utilizing Womenpower for National Development." Draft. EM3PH. Mimeo.

World Bank. 1989e. "Project Completion Report Malawi Fourth Education Project (Cr. 1123-MAI)." Rpt. No. 8195. Washington, D.C.

World Bank. 1989f. "Report of the President Mali Education Sector Consolidation Project." Rpt. No. P-5010-MLI. Washington, D.C.

World Bank. 1989g. "Staff Appraisal Report Djibouti Manpower and Education Development Project." Rpt. No. 8065-DJI. Washington, D.C.

World Bank. 1989h. "Staff Appraisal Report Morocco Rural Primary Education Project." Rpt. No. 7434-MOR. Washington, D.C.

World Bank. 1989i. Women in Pakistan -- An Economic and Social Strategy. Washington, D.C.

World Bank. 1989j. World Development Report.

World Bank. 1989k. World Tables 1989/90.

World Bank. 1990a. Bangladesh: Strategies for Enhancing the Role of Women in Economic Development. Washington, D.C.

World Bank. 1990b. Primary Education. A World Bank Policy Paper. Washington, D.C.

World Bank. 1990c. "Project Completion Report Bangladesh Fourth (Primary) Education Project (Cr. 1054-BD)." Rpt. No. 8355. Washington, D.C.

World Bank. 1990d. "Project Completion Report Papua New Guinea Primary Education Project (Cr. 1087-PNG/Ln. 1934.-PNG)." Rpt. No. 8968. Washington, D.C.

World Bank. 1990e. "Project Performance Audit Report Malawi: Third Education Project (Cr. 910-MAI), Fourth Education Project (Cr. 1123-MAI)." Rpt. No. 8480. Washington, D.C.

World Bank. 1990f. "Project Performance Audit Report Pakistan: Third Education Project (Cr. 678-PAK), Primary Education Project (Cr. 892-PAK) and Vocational Training Project (Cr. 1109-PAK)." Rpt. No. 8859. Washington, D.C.

World Bank. 1990g. "Report of the President Guinea Education Sector Adjustment Credit." Rpt. No. P-5288-GUI. Washington, D.C.

World Bank. 1990h. "Staff Appraisal Report Bangladesh General Education Project." Rpt. No. 8015-BD. Washington, D.C.

World Bank. 1990i. "Staff Appraisal Report The Gambia Education Sector Project." Rpt. No. 8359-GM. Washington, D.C.

World Bank. 1990j. "Staff Appraisal Report Madagascar Education Sector Reinforcement Project." Rpt. No. 8026-MAG. Washington, D.C.

World Bank. 1990k. "Staff Appraisal Report Nigeria Primary Education Project." Rpt. No. 8714-UNI. Washington, D.C.

World Bank. 1990l. "Staff Appraisal Report Pakistan Sindh Primary Education Development Program (FY91-95)". Rpt. No. 8178-PAK. Washington, D.C.

World Bank. 1990m. Women in Development: A Progress Report on the World Bank Initiative. Washington, D.C.

World Bank. 1990n. "Women in Development in Malawi: Constraints and Actions." AF6PH Draft. Mimeo.

World Bank. 1990o. World Development Report. Washington, D.C.

World Bank. 1991a. "Growth, Poverty Alleviation and Improved Income Distribution in Malaysia: Changing Focus of Government Policy Intervention." Economic Report. Washington, D.C.

World Bank. 1991b. "Staff Appraisal Report Morocco Rural Basic Education Development Project." Rpt. No. 8936-MOR. Washington, D.C.

World Bank. 1991c. "Zimbabwe Women in Development Strategy." Draft. PHRWD. Mimeo.

World Bank. 1991d. Gender and Poverty in India. Washington, D.C.

Appendix Table 1: RESULTS OF BANK-ASSISTED INTERVENTIONS TO IMPROVE FEMALE EDUCATION

REGION / PROJECT	INTERVENTIONS	RESULTS
AFRICA		
Malawi Second Education Cr. 590-MAI (1975-80) Cost $15.0 M. IDA credit $11.6 M. Rpt. 877	Additions to seven secondary schools (6 girls' schools, 1 co-ed) to increase the number of secondary school places available to girls, and improve the physical facilities of existing girls' schools. 1800 additional places to be created, 1600 for girls, with boarding facilities provided. Goal to raise female enrollment from 27.5% in 1975 to 35% by 1980.	Female enrollments in project schools rose from 27.5% in 1975 to only 29% by 1981. However, these were mainly transfers from government day schools (girls' enrollments in day schools fell by 2/3 while boarding school enrollments doubled), and places in day schools previously held by girls were taken up by boys. For the school system as a whole, the proportion of girls in secondary school rose only 0.5%. The overall quality of girls' education has improved with the addition of basic science facilities and workshop space. (PCR Rpt#4572, 1983)
Malawi Fourth Education Cr. 1123-MAI (1981-85) Cost $53.8 M. IDA credit $41.0 M. Rpt. 3183	Provision of 3,960 new secondary school places through 5 new schools and additions to 6 existing schools. In accord with Government policy, 1/3 of the places in the project schools would be reserved for girls. Therefore, 47% of new places for girls.	Girls' enrollments exceeded the target by 7%. However, a very uneven distribution of females in schools resulted, with vacancies in some and and overcrowding in others. (PCR Rpt#8195, 1989)
ASIA		
Bangladesh Fourth Primary, Cr. 1054-BD. (1980-86) Cost $52.42 M. IDA credit $40.0 M. Rpt. 2964	Classroom construction in new and existing schools to give access to 100,000 girls and 75,000 boys. School mapping to locate schools within acceptable walking distance from rural communities. Latrines and tubewells also provided at some schools. 500 female assistant teachers provided in primary schools. Provision of free uniforms for girls and free textbooks for all.	Female enrollment increased by 9% in project schools, compared to 1.8% in all primary schools. Female attrition rates also lower in project schools: reduced from 14 % in 1982 to 11% in 1984. Five hundred assistant teachers (mainly women) have been employed and are among those being trained in the in-service teacher training program. No evidence that the distribution of free uniforms contributed to a substantial increase in the enrollment of girls. There was a marginal increase in girls' enrollment at the start of the program, but enrollment decreased when some girls, although not eligible for free uniforms, dropped out of school because they were excluded from the program. Project was successful in raising overall enrollments. An important reason for the project's success seems to have been the introduction of several measures simultaneously. (PCR Rpt#8355, 1990)
Papua New Guinea First Education* Cr. 611-PNG. (1976-1981) Cost $7.4 M. IDA credit $4.0 M. Rpt. 1210	Expansion of Primary Teacher Training College, including boarding, with 2/3 of the 144 additional places for females. Hope to attract trainees, especially girls, from the Highland areas, who will return and help to relieve teacher shortages in the less developed areas.	Overall enrollments, including those of females, remained well below targets. This was due to an overestimate of the supply of female candidates. Social attitudes toward the education of girls substantially reduce the number of eligible females: only 35% of students in grades 7-10 are female. Thus, in 1980, of the 138 female graduates, only 4 were from the Highlands areas who returned home to teach. (Audit Rpt #5126, 1984)
Papua New Guinea Primary Educ., Cr. 1087-PNG. (1980-1988) Cost $12.0 M. IDA credit $6.0 M. Rpt. 3027b	Promote greater access to primary education through the creation of a Provincial Primary Education Fund (PPEF). The PPEF would help finance a variety of items identified as constraints to enrollment expansion in each province, especially for girls. Items to include physical facilities, equipment and materials, and experiments/studies to improve quality and access. 48% of girls were enrolled in primary school in 1979 vs. 68% of boys. Goal to reduce disparity and raise total primary enrollment to 68% from current 58%.	The formula for allocating PPEF funds among provinces targeted disadvantaged regions and the strategy has resulted in reduced interprovincial enrollment disparities. Female primary enrollments increased from 48% in 1987 to 68% in 1988. Policy interventions to raise girls' enrollments were developed at the provincial level; 8 provinces had projects specifically aimed at the education of girls. Specific innovations to raise female enrollments included hiring influential community members to monitor absenteeism (Community Liasion Helper Scheme), active support of girls' enrollment and retention through existing parent and community forums, and assigning of more female teachers to rural areas. (PCR Rpt#8968, 1990)

Appendix Table 1: RESULTS OF BANK-ASSISTED INTERVENTIONS TO IMPROVE FEMALE EDUCATION

REGION / PROJECT	INTERVENTIONS	RESULTS
Jordan First Education* Cr. 285-JO (1972-76) Cost $9.8 M. IDA credit $5.4 M. Rpt. PE-36a	Construction of coeducational Teacher Training Institute (TTI) for primary and preparatory teachers, 700 places.	875 trainees enrolled in the Teacher Training Institute. Female enrollments were greater than expected, comprising 60% of total. Objections against coeducation among some members of staff and community were outweighed by students' positive attitudes, and the flexibility and variety of programs. (Audit/PCR Rpt #2494, 1979)
Pakistan Third Education* Cr. 678-PAK (1977-1982) Cost $27.2 M. IDA credit $15.0 M. Rpt. 905	Establish 3 new female primary and secondary Teacher Training Institutes (TTIs); expansion and reconstruction in 7 existing. A 50% expansion in female teacher training capacity expected.	(Closed 1984) In 1984/85, enrollments in project female TTIs were 89% of appraisal capacity, compared with 64% of capacity in project male TTIs. However, the audit report found the management and maintenance of TTIs to be poor. (Audit Rpt#8859)
Pakistan Primary Educ. Cr. 892-PAK (1979-85) Cost: $17.2 M. IDA credit $10.0 M Rpt. 2305	Construction of classrooms in four provinces, 534 (53% of total number of classrooms) were for girls' schools and project activities were concentrated in areas most disadvantaged in terms of opportunities for girls. 288 residences for female teachers at new primary schools constructed under project. 340 assistant teachers, of which at least 190 (56%) females, recruited locally to teach in rural schools near their homes.	Although not part of original project design, boundary walls constructed around girls' schools. Success of this intervention measured by inclusion of boundary walls in subsequent Bank & donor projects for increasing girls' enrollments. Residences not successful in recruitment & retention of female teachers. Reasons included: social taboo and security risks for young women living alone especially in rural areas; housing allowance (up to 45% of salary) automatically deducted if women chose residence; and sometimes residences were used as classrooms where girls' schools were previously "shelterless" or constructed in open areas. Establishment of assistant teachers was successful in recruiting women. In general, for lack of gender-disaggregated data (a major omission of this project), there is no evidence of female enrollments improving as a result of project interventions. But this first primary education project has enabled new projects such as the Third Primary and Sindh projects to build on its experience by modifying interventions and and not repeating unsuccessful initiatives. (Audit Rpt#8859, 1990)
Syria First Education* Ln. 1480-SYR (1977-1984) Cost $40.3 M. IDA loan $20.5M. Rpt. 1513	Provision of 2,700 new places in 5 regional primary teacher training colleges (PTTC); half of new enrollments expected to be female. Provision of boarding facilities and monthly stipend expected to attract students from rural areas, especially girls, along with the policy of local posting.	Female enrollments exceeded projections, and male enrollments were significantly below projected rates. (2,441 females enrolled, vs. planned 1,360.) Boarding and dining facilities were deemed important in affecting parental decisions to send their daughters to project PTTCs. (Audit Rpt#5640, 1985)
Yemen Second Education* Cr. 611-YAR (1975-1981) Project Costs $12.3 M. IDA credit $8.0 M. Rpt. 970	In support of government policy to attract girls from remote areas, construction of 2 Primary Teacher Training Institutes (PTTIs) for girls with 560 new places and boarding for 140 girls. Also introduced double shift operations in 4 boys' PTTIs to accommodate girls.	Enrollment goals in girls' PTTIs reached. High internal efficiency with few dropouts and failures. Double shift at boys' PTTI did not work due to presence of male boarders on campus during girls' classes in afternoons. Boarding for girls was not succesful because of sociocultural factors; girls from outlying areas prefer to stay with relatives. (Audit Rpt#5086, 1984)

* Primary and Secondary Teacher Training Projects

Appendix Table 2: RECENT AND ONGOING BANK-ASSISTED INTERVENTIONS TO IMPROVE FEMALE EDUCATION

PROJECT/ (Cost)	Expand/build schools/ classrooms	Measures to alleviate distance problem	Curriculum reform/ removal of stereotypes	Flexible school hours/ calendar	Sanitary facilities/ tubewells/ boundary walls/ canteens	Measures to increase # of female teachers	Scholarships/ stipends for girls	Provision of textbooks/ abolish uniforms/ school feeding	Community campaigns/ local initiatives	Government policies/ plans to raise female enrollment	Data collection for monitoring/ pre-investment studies
Bangladesh **General Education (Rpt. 8015)** **Cr. 2118-BD (1990-96)** **($312.2M/IDA Cr. $159.3M)**		XX	XX	XX		XX	XX		XX		XX
Bangladesh **Second Primary Ed. (Rpt. 5362)** **Cr. 1574-BD (1985-91)** **($103.4M/IDA Cr. $78.0M)**	XX		XX		XX	XX					
Bhutan **Primary Education (Rpt. 7010)** **Cr. 1899-BHU (1988-93)** **($13.6M/IDA Cr. $4.2M)**		XX									XX
China **Teacher Training (Rpt. 7187)** **Cr. 1908-CHA (1988-93)** **($104.8M/IDA Cr. $50.0M)**						XX					XX
Djibouti **First Education (Rpt. 5215)** **Cr. 1543-DJI (1984-89)** **($7.4M/IDA Cr. $5.0M)**	XX (boarding)							XX			
Djibouti **Manpower and Ed. (Rpt. 8065)** **Cr. 2080-DJI (1990-95)** **($7.5M/IDA Cr. $5.8M)**							XX				
Ethiopia **Seventh Education (Rpt. 6931)** **Cr. 1878-ET (1987-95)** **($95.2M/IDA Cr.$70.0M)**						XX					
The Gambia **Education Sector (Rpt. 8359)** **Cr. 2142-GM (1990-96)** **($21.2M/IDA Cr. $14.6M)**	XX		XX			XX					XX
Guinea **Education Sector (Rpt. P-5288)** **Cr. 2155-GUI (1990-93)** **($44.0M/IDA Cr. $20.0M)**			XX								XX
Jordan **Sixth Education (Rpt. 4685)** **Ln. 2378-JO (1983-89)** **($122.0M/IDA Ln. $40.0M)**	XX										
Madagascar **Education Sector (Rpt. 8026)** **Cr. 2094-MAG (1990-96)** **($55.0M/IDA Cr. $39.0M)**										XX	
Malawi **Education Sector (Rpt. 6428)** **Cr. 1767-MAI (1987-90)** **($34.0M/IDA Cr. $27.0M)**	XX (boarding)									XX	
Maldives **Education & Training (Rpt. 7367** **Cr. 1981-MAL (1988-96)** **($9.3M/IDA Cr. $8.2M)**	XX										
Mali **Education Sector (Rpt. P-5010)** **Cr. 2054-MLI (1980-95)** **($56.2M/IDA Cr.$26.0M)**			XX								XX
Mauritania **Education Sector (Rpt. 7213)** **Cr. 1943-MAU (1988-93)** **($37.4M/IDA Cr. $18.2M)**										XX	

Appendix Table 2

PROJECT/ (Cost)	Expand/build schools/ classrooms	Measures to alleviate distance problem	Curriculum reform/ removal of stereotypes	Flexible school hours/ calendar	Sanitary facilities/ tubewells/ boundary walls/ canteens	Measures to increase # of female teachers	Scholarships/ stipends for girls	Provision of textbooks/ abolish uniforms/ school feeding	Community campaigns/ local initiatives	Government policies/ plans to raise female enrollment	Data collection for monitoring/ pre-investment studies
Morocco Rural Basic Ed. (Rpt. 8936) Rpt. 8936-MOR (1991-97) ($238.0/IBRD Ln. $145.0M)	XX (boarding)	XX					XX	XX			XX
Morocco Rural Primary Ed. (Rpt. 7434) Ln. 3026-MOR (1989-95) ($165.0M/IDA Ln. $83.0M)	XX	XX		XX	XX	XX		XX	XX		XX
Nigeria Primary Education (Rpt. 8714) Cr. 2191-UNI (1990-98) ($158.4M/IDA Cr.$120M)									XX		
Oman Second Education* (Rpt. 4958) Ln. 2419-OM (1984-90) ($23.9M/IDA Ln. $15.0M)	XX	XX									
Oman Third Education* (Rpt. 6584) Ln. 2799-OM (1987-95) ($27.7M/IDA Ln.$13.8M)	XX	XX				XX					
Pakistan Sindh Education (Rpt. 8178) Cr. 2102-PAK (1990-95) ($196.4M/IDA Cr. $145.0M)	XX	XX		XX	XX	XX	XX	XX			XX
Pakistan Second Primary Ed. (Rpt. 5363) Cr. 1602-PAK (1985-92) ($73.0M/IDA Cr. $52.5M)						XX					
Pakistan Third Primary Ed. (Rpt. 6492) Cr. 1821-PAK (1987-94) ($446.0M/IDA Cr.$145.0M)	XX		XX	XX	XX	XX	XX	XX	XX		XX
Solomon Islands Secondary Education* (Rpt. 564 Cr. 1686-SOL (1986-92) ($10.0/IDA Cr. $5.0M)	XX (boarding)										
Tanzania Seventh Education (Rpt. 2782) Cr. 1056-TA (1980-86) ($55.5M/IDA Cr. $25.0M)	XX		XX								
Yemen Fifth Education* (Rpt. 4223) Cr. 1340-YAR (1983-89) ($19.3M/IDA Cr. $10.0M))						XX					
Yemen Sixth Education (Rpt. 4634) Cr. 1470-YAR (1984-90) ($20.1M/IDA Cr.$10.0M)						XX					
Yemen Teacher Training (Rpt. 6463) Cr. 1733-YAR (1987-93) ($20.1M/IDA Cr. $10.4M)						XX					

*Primary and Secondary Teacher Training

ANNEX A: TECHNICAL NOTES AND STATISTICAL TABLES

Table A-1.

The total primary enrollment ratios for boys and girls are expressed as the number of boys and girls enrolled in primary school as a percentage of the respective populations of school-age boys and girls. Many countries consider primary school age to be 6 to 11, but some do not. The differences in country practices in the ages and duration of schooling are reflected in these ratios. For some countries with universal primary education, these numbers may exceed 100 because some pupils are younger or older than the country's standard school age. For the years 1975 to 1985 the data are taken from the *Bank Economic and Social Database* which uses mostly UNESCO data for education. For 1987 the data are from UNESCO Statistical Yearbook, 1990.

Table A-2.

The total secondary enrollment ratios for boys and girls show the number of boys and girls enrolled in secondary school as a percentage of the respective populations of school age boys and girls. Again, the definition of secondary school age differs among countries but is most commonly considered to be 12 to 17. The sources are the same as for Table A-1.

Table A-3.

The number of females per 100 males in primary and secondary school measures gender parity in enrollment rates. This ratio expresses the female enrollment rate as a percentage of the male enrollment rate based on the data in Tables A-1 (primary) and A-2 (secondary). Numbers below 100 indicate a gap from parity; numbers above 100 indicate a female enrollment rate higher than the male rate. Other things being equal, if opportunities for both sexes were equal, the ratio should be close to 100. In reality, however, inequalities in access may cause the ratio to move in different directions. For example, the ratio will rise at the secondary level if male attendance declines more rapidly in the final grades because of greater job opportunities, conscription into the army, or migration in search of work. Yet it generally falls well below 100. The reasons are discussed in Chapter 3.

Table A-4.

The amount of government spending on education represents central government spending on all public education; it does not include local (district, state, etc.) expenditures. The data are from UNESCO Yearbooks which report the amounts and then calculate the percentages of the total government expenditure, and of World Bank GNP figures. The earliest year reported in the most recent yearbook (1990) is 1975; earlier years are from the 1979 yearbook.

Table A-5.

Per capita gross national income is the sum of per capita GNP and the terms of trade adjustment -- using 1980 as a base year for comparison over time. The data are from the World Bank World Tables, 1989/90. Per capita GNP (1987) is from the World Development Report, 1989.

Table A-1. **Primary School Enrollment Rates**

	Percentage of age group enrolled											
	Male						Female					
	1965	1970	1975	1980	1985	1987	1965	1970	1975	1980	1985	1987
Africa (32):												
Benin	48	51	70	88	87	84	21	22	31	40	43	43
Botswana	59	63	65	84	103	111	71	67	79	100	112	117
Burkina Faso	16	17	21	23	36	41	8	10	12	14	21	24
Burundi	36	42	28	35	61	68	15	20	17	22	44	50
Cameroon	114	103	108	113	117	119	75	75	87	94	98	100
Central African R.	84	88	96	93	94	82	28	41	51	51	59	51
Chad	56	52	51	.	63	73	13	17	18	.	24	29
Cote d'Ivoire	80	71	77	89	82	.	41	45	47	59	58	.
Ethiopia	16	23	32	45	40	46	6	10	15	25	27	28
Ghana	82	73	80	89	.	78	57	54	62	71	.	63
Guinea	44	45	40	42	42	41	19	21	20	21	19	18
Kenya	69	67	103	120	101	98	40	48	87	110	96	93
Lesotho	74	71	87	85	101	102	114	101	123	120	125	127
Madagascar	70	99	103	146	.	97	59	82	88	139	.	92
Malawi	55	.	.	72	70	73	32	.	.	48	53	59
Mali	32	30	32	34	29	29	16	15	17	19	17	17
Mauritania	19	20	24	47	60	61	6	8	13	26	39	42
Mauritius	105	94	108	108	105	105	97	93	106	108	106	107
Mozambique	48	.	.	115	97	76	26	.	.	84	75	59
Niger	15	19	25	35	36	37	7	10	14	19	20	20
Nigeria	39	47	.	110	.	72	24	27	.	84	.	56
Rwanda	64	76	61	66	64	69	43	60	51	60	61	66
Senegal	52	51	48	55	69	71	29	32	34	36	46	49
Sierra Leone	37	40	47	61	.	68	23	27	30	43	.	48
Somalia	16	17	76	35	20	.	4	5	42	19	10	.
Sudan	37	47	59	56	58	59	21	29	34	41	41	41
Tanzania	40	41	62	100	73	67	25	27	44	86	71	66
Togo	78	98	130	151	118	124	32	44	68	93	73	78
Uganda	83	46	53	56	.	76	50	30	35	43	.	63
Zaire	95	110	104	109	106	86	45	65	72	79	70	65
Zambia	59	99	105	98	106	102	46	80	88	82	93	92
Zimbabwe	128	81	79	.	140	130	92	66	67	.	131	126
Asia (17):												
Bangladesh	67	72	95	76	70	76	31	35	51	46	50	64
Bhutan	13	11	.	.	34	31	1	1	.	.	19	20
China	.	.	135	121	132	140	.	.	115	103	114	124
Hong Kong	.	118	122	107	105	106	99	115	117	105	103	105
India	86	90	94	98	110	113	57	56	62	67	79	81
Indonesia	79	87	94	115	121	120	65	73	78	100	114	115
Korea, Rep.	103	104	107	109	96	104	99	103	107	111	97	104
Lao, P.D.R.	50	66	.	123	121	102	30	40	.	104	100	85
Malaysia	96	91	92	93	101	102	84	84	89	92	100	102
Nepal	36	44	86	122	.	104	4	8	16	52	.	47
Pakistan	59	57	63	51	67	51	20	22	28	27	36	28
Papua New Guinea	53	63	68	66	.	75	35	39	43	51	.	64
Philippines	115	.	.	113	106	105	111	.	.	113	107	107
Singapore	110	109	113	109	.	118	100	101	107	106	.	113
Sri Lanka	98	104	81	105	104	105	86	94	74	100	101	102
Thailand	82	86	87	100	.	.	74	79	80	97	.	.
Vietnam	.	.	106	111	105	.	.	.	108	106	99	.
Latin America (21):												
Argentina	101	105	106	106	107	110	102	106	106	106	108	110
Bolivia	86	91	94	90	.	97	60	62	76	78	.	85
Brazil	109	.	89	101	.	.	108	.	87	97	.	.
Chile	125	107	119	110	107	103	122	107	118	108	104	101
Colombia	83	107	116	127	116	112	86	110	120	130	119	115
Costa Rica	107	110	108	106	98	100	105	109	106	104	96	97
Dominican Rep.	87	100	.	.	121	99	87	100	.	.	126	103
Ecuador	94	99	106	115	115	118	88	95	102	111	116	116
El Salvador	85	87	76	75	.	77	79	83	74	75	.	81
Guatemala	55	62	67	77	83	82	45	51	56	65	70	70
Haiti	56	.	.	79	101	83	44	.	.	68	89	72
Honduras	81	87	89	92	101	104	79	87	86	94	103	108
Jamaica	112	119	97	100	.	104	106	119	98	101	.	106
Mexico	94	106	112	116	120	119	90	101	106	115	117	116
Nicaragua	68	79	80	96	96	94	69	81	85	102	107	104
Panama	104	101	116	108	107	109	99	97	111	104	102	104
Paraguay	109	115	106	107	105	104	96	103	97	101	100	99

Table A-1. Primary School Enrollment Rates (continued)

	Percentage of age group enrolled											
	Male						Female					
	1965	1970	1975	1980	1985	1987	1965	1970	1975	1980	1985	1987
Latin America (cont.):												
Peru	108	114	.	117	125	125	90	99	.	111	120	120
Trinidad & Tobago	97	106	97	94	93	99	90	107	100	101	96	100
Uruguay	106	115	107	107	111	111	106	109	106	106	109	109
Venezuela	93	94	97	.	109	107	94	94	97	.	108	100
Middle East (17):												
Afghanistan	26	47	44	54	27	27	5	8	8	12	13	14
Algeria	81	93	109	108	103	105	53	58	75	81	82	87
Egypt	90	87	85	90	96	100	60	57	57	65	87	79
Iran	85	93	114	.	117	122	40	52	71	.	97	105
Iraq	102	95	122	120	108	105	45	41	64	109	92	91
Jordan	105	.	.	105	.	98	83	.	.	102	.	99
Kuwait	129	101	99	104	98	95	103	76	85	100	94	92
Lebanon	118	113	.	.	.	105	93	112	.	.	.	95
Morocco	78	66	78	96	94	85	35	36	45	59	60	56
Oman	.	6	63	77	97	103	.	1	24	42	80	92
Saudi Arabia	36	61	72	75	77	78	11	29	43	50	61	65
Syria	103	95	112	114	115	115	52	59	78	89	101	104
Tunisia	116	121	116	118	126	126	65	79	78	88	106	107
Turkey	118	124	.	102	117	121	83	94	.	90	110	113
U. Arab Emirates	.	112	104	89	95	98	.	71	97	88	95	100
Yemen, A.R.	16	23	50	79	130	141	1	2	7	12	33	40
Yemen, P.D.R.	.	91	109	93	.	96	.	23	51	36	.	35

Source: Unesco data; see Technical Note for full reference.

Table A-2. Secondary School Enrollment Rates

	Percentage of age group enrolled											
	Male						Female					
	1965	1970	1975	1980	1985	1987	1965	1970	1975	1980	1985	1987
Africa (32):												
Benin	5	6	13	25	25	23	2	3	5	9	10	9
Botswana	5	9	16	20	29	31	3	6	16	22	31	33
Burkina Faso	2	2	3	4	6	8	1	1	1	2	3	4
Burundi	2	3	4	4	5	6	1	1	2	2	3	3
Cameroon	8	11	17	24	29	26	2	4	8	13	18	19
Central African R.	4	7	13	21	24	17	1	2	3	7	8	6
Chad	3	4	.	.	.	10	0	0.3	.	.	.	2
Côte d'Ivoire	10	13	18	26	27	26	2	4	7	11	11	12
Ethiopia	3	6	9	11	16	18	1	2	4	6	11	12
Ghana	19	21	45	51	.	49	7	8	28	31	.	32
Guinea	9	21	20	21	15	13	2	5	7	8	5	4
Kenya	6	12	16	23	26	27	2	5	9	16	16	19
Lesotho	4	7	12	14	.	18	4	7	14	20	.	26
Madagascar	10	14	14	.	.	23	5	9	10	.	.	19
Malawi	3	.	.	5	6	5	1	.	.	2	2	3
Mali	5	8	11	13	9	9	2	2	3	5	4	4
Mauritania	2	4	.	18	23	23	0	0.4	.	4	8	9
Mauritius	34	35	42	50	53	53	18	25	35	47	49	50
Mozambique	3	.	.	8	10	7	2	.	.	3	4	4
Niger	1	2	3	7	8	9	0	1	1	3	3	4
Nigeria	5	6	3	24	.	29	3	3	.	13	.	18
Rwanda	3	3	3	4	7	7	1	1	1	3	5	5
Senegal	10	14	.	15	18	19	3	6	.	7	9	10
Sierra Leone	8	12	16	20	26	.	3	5	7	8	12	.
Somalia	4	8	9	15	12	.	1	2	3	5	6	.
Sudan	6	10	19	20	23	23	2	4	8	12	17	17
Tanzania	3	4	4	4	4	5	1	2	2	2	2	3
Togo	8	11	29	.	33	36	2	3	9	.	10	12
Uganda	6	6	6	7	.	16	2	2	2	3	.	9
Zaire	8	13	23	49	.	32	2	4	8	18	.	14
Zambia	11	17	20	22	23	.	3	8	10	11	13	.
Zimbabwe	8	9	10	.	50	49	5	6	7	.	33	42
Asia (17):												
Bangladesh	23	.	40	26	26	24	3	.	11	9	10	11
Bhutan	0	1	2	.	6	7	0	0.04	0.3	.	1	2
China	.	.	55	54	45	50	.	.	38	37	32	37
Hong Kong	32	40	51	63	70	71	25	31	47	65	75	76
India	41	36	36	41	49	50	13	15	16	22	27	27
Indonesia	18	21	25	35	.	53	7	11	15	23	.	42
Korea, Rep.	44	50	64	81	92	91	25	32	48	71	87	86
Lao, PDR	2	5	.	25	27	23	1	2	.	16	19	16
Malaysia	34	40	46	50	52	59	22	28	38	46	53	59
Nepal	9	16	23	33	.	35	2	3	4	9	.	11
Pakistan	18	20	22	20	23	26	5	5	7	8	8	11
Papua New Guinea	6	11	16	15	.	16	2	4	7	8	.	9
Philippines	42	.	.	61	63	66	40	.	.	69	66	66
Singapore	49	47	51	56	.	70	41	45	52	59	.	73
Sri Lanka	34	46	47	53	60	63	35	48	49	57	67	69
Thailand	16	20	28	30	.	30	11	15	23	28	.	28
Vietnam	.	.	38	44	43	.	.	.	41	40	40	.
Latin America (21):												
Argentina	26	42	5	.	66	69	31	47	57	.	75	78
Bolivia	21	28	.	41	.	40	15	20	.	31	.	35
Brazil	16	25	24	31	32	32	16	26	28	36	41	41
Chile	31	36	45	49	64	72	36	42	52	56	70	76
Colombia	18	25	39	43	50	55	16	24	39	45	51	56
Costa Rica	23	27	40	44	38	40	25	29	45	51	42	43
Dominican Rep.	11	.	.	.	44	.	12	.	.	.	57	.
Ecuador	19	21	41	51	54	54	16	23	38	51	56	57
El Salvador	18	23	21	26	.	27	17	21	17	23	.	30
Guatemala	10	9	12	20	.	.	7	8	11	17	.	.
Haiti	6	.	8	14	18	19	3	.	7	12	16	17
Honduras	11	14	16	29	.	.	9	13	17	30	.	.
Jamaica	53	46	53	55	.	62	50	45	63	63	.	67
Mexico	21	27	41	48	54	54	13	17	28	43	52	53
Nicaragua	15	19	23	40	23	29	13	17	24	46	55	58
Panama	32	36	52	58	56	56	36	40	57	64	63	63
Paraguay	13	17	20	.	31	30	13	17	20	.	30	30

Table A-2. Secondary School Enrollment Rates (continued)

	Percentage of age group enrolled											
	Male						*Female*					
	1965	*1970*	*1975*	*1980*	*1985*	*1987*	*1965*	*1970*	*1975*	*1980*	*1985*	*1987*
Latin America (cont.):												
Peru	29	35	50	63	68	68	21	27	41	54	61	61
Trinidad & Tobago	39	40	45	.	.	80	34	44	51	.	.	85
Uruguay	42	54	.	59	.	.	46	64	.	61	.	.
Venezuela	27	33	40	36	41	48	28	34	45	45	50	59
Middle East (17):												
Afghanastan	4	13	13	16	12	10	1	2	2	4	6	5
Algeria	10	16	26	40	59	61	5	6	14	26	43	48
Egypt	37	46	54	65	77	79	15	23	31	41	54	58
Iran	24	36	57	.	53	57	11	18	33	.	36	39
Iraq	42	34	48	75	69	60	14	14	21	38	39	38
Jordan	52	.	.	79	.	80	23	.	.	73	.	78
Kuwait	59	69	71	84	89	86	43	57	61	76	82	79
Lebanon	33	49	.	.	.	57	20	33	.	.	.	56
Morocco	16	17	21	32	40	43	5	7	12	19	27	30
Oman	.	.	2	21	43	46	.	.	0.5	7	22	29
Saudi Arabia	7	19	28	36	51	52	1	5	15	23	33	35
Syria	43	54	57	58	71	69	13	21	28	36	49	48
Tunisia	23	33	28	34	46	46	9	13	15	20	32	34
Turkey	22	38	40	44	52	57	9	15	19	24	30	34
U. Arab Emirates	.	30	36	56	52	55	.	9	29	48	63	66
Yemen, A.R.	.	2	8	9	28	46	.	0.1	1	1	3	6
Yemen, P.D.R.	.	16	36	25	.	26	.	4	10	11	.	11

Source: Unesco data; see Technical Note for full reference.

Table A-3. Females per 100 Males in Primary and Secondary Schools

	Female enrollment rate as a percentage of male enrollment rate											
	Primary						Secondary					
	1965	1970	1975	1980	1985	1987	1965	1970	1975	1980	1985	1987
Africa (32):												
Benin	43.8	43.1	44.3	45.5	49.4	51.2	40.0	50.0	38.5	36.0.	40.0	39.1
Botswana	120.3	106.3	121.5	119.0	108.7	105.4	60.0	66.7	100.0	110.0	106.9	106.5
Burkina Faso	50.0	58.8	57.1	60.9	58.3	58.5	50.0	50.0	33.3	50.0	60.0	50.0
Burundi	41.7	47.6	60.7	62.9	72.1	73.5	50.0	33.3	50.0	50.0	60.0	50.0
Cameroon	65.8	72.8	80.6	83.2	83.8	84.0	25.0	36.4	47.1	54.2	62.1	62.5
C.A.R.	33.3	46.6	53.1	54.8	62.8	62.2	25.0	28.6	23.1	33.3	33.3	35.3
Chad	23.2	32.7	35.3	.	38.1	39.7	0.0	7.5	.	.	.	20.0
Côte d'Ivoire	51.2	63.4	61.0	66.3	70.7	.	20.0	38.8	38.9	42.3	40.7	46.2
Ethiopia	37.5	43.5	46.9	55.6	67.5	60.9	33.3	33.3	44.4	54.5	68.8	66.7
Ghana	69.5	74.0.	77.5	79.8	.	80.8	36.8	38.1	62.2	60.8	.	65.3
Guinea	43.2	46.7	50.0	50.0	45.2	43.9	22.2	23.8	35.0	38.1	33.3	30.8
Kenya	58.0	71.6	84.5	91.7	95.0	94.9	33.3	41.7	56.3	69.6	61.5	70.4
Lesotho	154.1	142.3	141.4	141.2	123.8	124.5	100.0	100.0	116.7	142.9	.	144.4
Madagascar	84.3	82.8	85.4	95.2	.	94.8	50.0	64.3	71.4	.	.	82.6
Malawi	58.2	.	.	66.7	75.7	80.8	33.3	.	.	40.4	33.3	60.0
Mali	50.0	50.0	53.1	55.9	58.6	58.6	40.0	25.0	27.3	38.5	44.4	44.4
Mauritania	31.6	40.0	54.2	55.3	65.0	68.9	0.0	11.0	.	22.2	34.8	39.1
Mauritius	92.4	98.9	98.1	100.0	101.0	101.9	52.9	71.4	83.3	94.0	92.5	94.3
Mozambique	54.2	.	.	73.0	77.3	77.6	66.7	.	.	37.5	40.0	57.1
Niger	46.7	52.6	56.0	54.3	55.6	54.1	0.0	50.0	33.3	42.9	37.5	44.4
Nigeria	61.5	57.4	.	76.4	.	77.8	60.0	50.0	.	54.2	.	62.1
Rwanda	67.2	78.9	83.6	90.9	95.3	95.7	33.3	33.3	33.3	75.0	71.4	71.4
Senegal	55.8	62.7	70.8	65.5	66.7	69.0	30.0	42.9	.	46.7	50.0	52.6
Sierra Leone	62.2	67.5	63.8	70.5	.	70.6	37.5	41.7	43.8	40.0	46.2	.
Somalia	25.0	29.4	55.3	54.3	50.0	50.0	25.0	25.0	33.3	33.3	50.0	.
Sudan	56.8	61.7	57.6	69.5	70.7	69.5	33.3	40.0	42.1	60.0	73.9	73.9
Tanzania	62.5	65.9	71.0	86.0	97.3	98.5	33.3	50.0	50.0	50.0	50.0	60.0
Togo	41.0	44.9	52.3	61.6	61.9	62.9	25.0	27.3	31.0	.	30.3	33.3
Uganda	60.2	65.2	66.0	76.8	.	82.9	33.3	33.3	33.3	42.9	.	56.3
Zaire	47.4	59.1	69.2	72.5	66.0	75.6	25.0	30.8	34.8	36.7	.	43.8
Zambia	78.0	80.8	83.8	83.7	87.7	90.2	27.3	47.1	50.0	50.0	56.5	56.5
Zimbabwe	71.9	81.5	84.8	.	93.6	96.9	62.5	66.7	70.0	.	66.0	85.7
Asia (17):												
Bangladesh	46.3	48.6	53.7	60.5	71.4	84.2	13.0	.	27.5	34.6	38.5	45.8
Bhutan	7.7	9.1	.	.	55.9	64.5	.	4.0	15.0	.	16.7	28.6
China	.	.	85.2	85.1	86.4	88.6	.	.	69.1	68.5	71.1	74.0
Hong Kong	.	97.5	95.9	98.1	98.1	99.1	78.1	77.5	92.2	103.2	107.1	107.0
India	64.0	62.2	66.0	68.4	71.8	71.7	31.7	41.7	44.4	53.7	55.1	54.1
Indonesia	82.3	83.9	83.0	87.0	94.2	95.8	38.9	52.4	60.0	65.7	.	79.2
Korea, Rep.	96.1	99.0	100.0	101.8	101.0	100.0	56.8	64.0	75.0	87.7	94.6	94.5
Lao, P.D.R.	60.0	60.6	.	84.6	82.6	83.3	50.0	40.0	.	64.0	70.4	69.6
Malaysia	87.5	92.3	96.7	98.9	99.0	100.0	67.7	70.0	82.6	92.0	101.9	100.0
Nepal	11.1	18.2	18.6	42.6	.	45.2	22.2	18.8	17.4	27.3	.	31.4
Pakistan	33.9	38.6	44.4	52.9	54.5	54.9	27.8	25.0	31.8	40.0	34.8	42.3
Papua New Guinea	66.0	61.9	63.2	77.3	.	85.3	33.3	36.4	43.8	53.3	.	56.3
Philippines	96.5	.	.	100.0	100.9	101.9	95.2	.	.	113.1	104.8	100.0
Singapore	90.9	92.7	94.7	97.2	.	95.8	83.7	95.7	102.0	105.4	.	104.3
Sri Lanka	87.8	90.4	91.4	9532	97.1	97.1	101.9	104.3	104.3	107.5	111.7	109.5
Thailand	90.2	91.9	92.0	97.0	.	.	68.8	75.0	82.1	93.3	.	.
Vietnam	.	.	107.9	90.9	93.0	.	.	.	101.9	95.5	94.3	.
Latin America (21):												
Argentina	101.0	101.0	100.0	100.0	100.9	100.0	119.2	111.9	1140.0	.	113.6	113.0
Bolivia	69.8	68.1	80.9	86.7	.	87.6	71.4	71.4	.	75.6	.	87.5
Brazil	99.1	.	97.8	96.0	.	.	100.0	104.0	116.7	116.1	126.1	128.1
Chile	97.6	100.0	99.2	98.2	97.2	98.1	116.1	116.7	115.6	114.3	109.4	105.6
Colombia	103.6	102.8	103.4	102.4	102.6	102.7	88.9	96.0	100.0	104.7	102.0	101.8
Costa Rica	98.1	99.1	98.1	98.1	98.0	97.0	108.7	107.4	112.5	115.9	110.5	107.5
Dominican Rep.	100.0	100.0	.	.	104.1	104.0	109.1	.	.	.	129.5	.
Ecuador	93.6	96.0	96.2	96.5	98.3	98.3	84.2	109.5	92.7	100.0	103.7	103.6
El Salvador	92.9	95.4	97.4	100.0		105.2	94.4	91.3	81.0	88.5	.	111.1
Guatemala	81.8	82.3	83.6	84.4	84.3	85.4	70.0	88.9	91.7	85.0	.	85.0
Haiti	78.6	.	.	86.1	88.1	86.7	50.0	.	87.5	85.7	88.9	89.5
Honduras	97.5	100.0	96.6	102.2	102.0	103.8	81.8	92.9	106.3	103.4	.	120.7
Jamaica	94.6	100.0	101.0	101.0	.	101.9	94.3	97.8	118.9	114.5	.	108.1
Mexico	95.7	95.3	94.6	99.1	97.5	97.5	61.9	63.0	98.3	89.6	96.3	98.1
Nicaragua	101.5	102.5	106.3	106.3	111.5	110.6	86.7	89.5	104.3	115.0	239.1	200.0
Panama	95.2	96.0	95.7	96.3	95.3	95.4	112.5	111.1	109.6	110.3	112.5	112.5
Paraguay	88.1	89.6	91.5	94.4	95.2	95.2	100.0	100.0	100.0	.	96.8	100.0

Table A-3. Females per 100 Males in Primary and Secondary Schools (continued)

	Female enrollment rate as a percentage of male enrollment rate											
	Primary						Secondary					
	1965	*1970*	*1975*	*1980*	*1985*	*1987*	*1965*	*1970*	*1975*	*1980*	*1985*	*1987*
Latin America (cont.):												
Peru	83.3	86.8	.	94.9	96.0	96.0	72.4	77.1	82.0	85.7	89.7	89.7
Trinidad & Tobago	92.8	100.9	103.1	107.4	103.2	101.0	87.2	100.0	113.3	.	.	106.3
Uruguay	100.0	94.8	99.1	99.1	98.2	98.2	109.5	118.5	.	103.4	.	103.4
Venezuela	101.1	100.0	100.0	.	99.1	100.0	103.7	103.0	112.5	125.0	122.0	122.9
Middle East (17):												
Afghanistan	19.2	17.0	18.2	22.2	48.1	51.9	25.0	15.4	15.4	25.0	50.0	50.0
Algeria	65.4	62.4	68.8	75.0	79.6	82.9	50.0	37.5	53.8	65.0	72.9	75.4
Egypt	66.7	65.5	67.1	72.2	81.3	79.0	40.5	50.0	57.4	63.1	70.1	73.4
Iran	47.1	55.9	62.3	.	82.9	86.1	45.8	50.0	57.9	.	67.9	68.4
Iraq	44.1	43.2	52.5	90.8	85.2	86.7	33.3	41.2	43.8	50.7	56.5	63.3
Jordan	79.0	.	.	97.1	.	101.0	44.2	.	.	92.4	.	97.5
Kuwait	79.8	75.2	85.9	96.2	95.9	96.8	72.9	82.6	85.9	90.5	92.1	91.9
Lebanon	78.8	86.2	.	.	.	90.5	60.6	67.3	.	.	.	98.2
Morocco	44.9	54.5	57.7	61.5	63.8	65.9	31.3	41.2	54.1	59.4	67.5	69.8
Oman	.	16.7	38.1	54.5	82.5	89.3	.	.	23.0	33.3	51.2	63.0
Saudi Arabia	30.6	47.5	59.7	66.7	79.2	83.3	14.3	26.3	53.6	63.9	64.7	67.3
Syria	50.5	62.1	69.6	78.1	87.8	90.4	30.2	38.9	49.1	62.1	69.0	69.6
Tunisia	56.0	65.3	67.2	74.6	84.1	84.9	39.1	39.4	53.6	58.8	69.6	73.9
Turkey	70.3	75.8	.	88.2	94.0	93.4	40.9	39.5	47.5	54.5	57.7	59.6
U. Arab Emirates	.	63.4	93.3	98.9	100.0	102.0	.	30.0	80.6	85.7	121.2	120.0
Yemen, A.R.	6.3	8.7	14.0	15.2	25.4	28.4	.	5.0	12.5	11.1	10.7	13.0
Yemen, P.D.R.	.	25.3	46.8	38.7	.	36.5	.	25.0	27.8	44.0	.	42.3

Source: calculated from Tables A-1 and A-2 which are from Unesco data; see Technical Note for full reference.

Table A-4. Government Spending on Education

	Total central government spending on education											
	as a % of GNP						*as a % of total government exp.*					
	1965	*1970*	*1975*	*1980*	*1985*	*1987*	*1965*	*1970*	*1975*	*1980*	*1985*	*1987*
Africa (32):												
Benin	3.8	4.2	.	.	.	.	26.8	29.7	.	.	.	.
Botswana	4.4	4.8	8.5	7.1	7.7	7.7	10.1	12.3	18.8	16.0	15.4	14.4
Burkina Faso	2.1	2.3	2.5	2.6	2.5	.	18.2	25.9	.	19.8	21.0	.
Burundi	2.0	2.3	.	3.0	2.6	2.9	20.0	25.8	.	17.5	15.5	.
Cameroon	3.6	3.8	3.9	3.2	3.7	2.7	18.0	19.6	21.3	20.3	18.9	17.8
Central Arab R.	2.7	3.1	4.9	.	2.6	2.9	16.5	16.1	20.1	.	.	16.8
Chad	2.6	2.6	.	.	.	.	17.9	13.0	.	.	.	.
Côte d'Ivoire	5.0	6.7	6.6	6.9	.	.	19.8	19.3	19.1	.	.	.
Ethiopia	1.3	2.8	3.3	3.3	4.2	.	8.8	14.1	14.5	10.4	9.5	9.9
Ghana	4.5	4.3	5.9	3.1	2.6	3.4	17.7	19.6	21.5	.	.	.
Guinea	.	.	.	.	3.3	.	23.8	28.3	.	.	15.3	.
Kenya	4.6	4.1	6.3	6.9	6.5	7.0	18.3	17.6	19.4	18.1	.	22.7
Lesotho	3.8	3.5	4.5	5.0	3.6	.	15.1	.	23.5	14.8	.	.
Madagascar	6.3	3.6	3.2	5.4	3.5	.	27.0	14.8	18.5	.	.	.
Malawi	3.6	4.0	2.4	3.3	3.5	3.3	15.4	13.2	9.6	.	8.5	.
Mali	4.5	.	.	3.7	3.7	3.2	.	11.5	.	30.8	.	17.3
Mauritania	1.9	3.8	3.8	.	.	.	14.1	21.9	.	.	.	.
Mauritius	3.3	3.7	3.6	5.3	3.8	3.5	11.9	11.5	9.6	11.6	9.8	10.0
Mozambique	0.6	0.8	.	.	.	.	3.9	5.7	.	.	.	.
Niger	1.2	2.0	2.4	3.1	.	.	12.0	17.7	18.7	22.9	.	.
Nigeria	2.4	2.5	2.9	5.5	1.0	1.4	20.7	20.0	.	.	8.7	12.0
Rwanda	2.6	2.6	2.6	2.7	3.4	3.5	23.4	26.6	25.3	21.6	.	22.3
Senegal	3.2	3.9	.	.	.	.	19.0	21.3	.	.	.	.
Sierra Leone	3.6	3.2	3.4	3.8	.	.	.	17.5	.	.	.	.
Somalia	1.4	1.8	2.1	1.0	.	.	6.9	7.6	12.5	8.7	.	.
Sudan	2.7	2.9	5.5	4.8	.	.	15.8	12.6	14.8	9.1	.	.
Tanzania	.	.	5.4	5.1	4.2	4.1	23.7	16.0	17.8	14.3	19.0	9.7
Togo	2.0	2.2	3.5	5.6	5.3	5.1	15.1	18.6	.	.	.	.
Uganda	3.8	3.9	2.5	1.2	2.7	3.9	18.6	17.6	17.0	11.3	.	22.5
Zaire	3.4	6.1	.	.	.	.	16.0	20.4	.	.	.	.
Zambia	5.2	4.5	6.7	4.5	5.4	.	17.6	10.9	11.9	7.6	16.3	.
Zimbabwe	3.4	3.3	3.6	6.6	8.5	.	16.8	16.2	.	13.7	16.0	16.2
Asia (14):												
Bangladesh	1.3	.	1.1	1.5	1.9	2.2	14.4	.	13.6	8.2	.	10.5
China			1.8	2.5	2.7	.	.	2.9	4.2	6.1	.	.
India	2.5	2.8	2.5	2.5	3.3	3.4	8.7	10.7	8.6	10.0	9.4	.
Indonesia	.	2.5	2.7	1.7	.	.	.	.	13.1	8.9	.	.
Korea, Rep.	1.8	3.7	2.2	3.7	4.8	4.2	17.2	21.4	13.9	23.7	28.2	26.6
Lao, P.D.R	.	.	.	.	1.0	.	8.1	10.8	.	1.3	4.5	6.6
Malaysia	4.7	4.3	6.0	6.0	6.6	7.0	18.5	17.3	19.3	14.7	16.3	.
Nepal	0.6	0.6	1.5	1.8	2.8	.	8.2	6.7	11.5	12.4	10.8	.
Pakistan	1.8	1.7	2.2	2.0	2.2	2.1	5.3	4.2	5.2	5.0	.	.
Papua New G.	.	.	.	.	.	.	14.4	13.2	.	.	.	.
Philippines	2.6	2.7	1.9	1.6	1.3	2.0	.	24.4	11.4	10.3	7.0	.
Singapore	4.3	3.1	2.9	2.8	.	3.8	.	11.7	8.6	7.3	.	11.5
Sri Lanka	4.5	4.3	2.8	3.1	3.1	3.8	14.7	13.6	10.1	8.8	8.0	.
Thailand	.	.	3.5	3.4	3.9	3.6	20.1	17.3	21.0	20.6	18.5	17.9
Latin America (21):												
Argentina	2.9	3.3	2.5	3.6	2.0	1.9	.	16.8	9.5	15.1	8.6	8.9
Bolivia	2.6	4.7	3.5	4.4	0.4	.	24.7	28.4	.	25.3	.	.
Brazil	2.4	2.7	3.0	3.5	3.7	4.5	11.9	10.6	.	.	19.1	17.7
Chile	3.4	5.1	4.1	4.6	4.4	3.6	15.1	22.0	12.0	11.9	15.3	.
Colombia	2.3	3.2	2.2	1.9	2.8	2.7	13.9	13.6	16.4	14.3	24.7	22.4
Costa Rica	4.6	5.2	6.8	7.8	4.5	4.6	29.0	31.8	31.1	22.2	22.7	21.6
Dominican Rep.	2.7	2.9	2.1	2.3	1.8	1.6	14.5	15.9	14.3	16.0	14.0	10.0
Ecuador	.	.	3.2	5.6	3.7	3.5	.	23.2	25.9	33.3	20.6	21.3
El Salvador	2.8	2.8	3.4	3.9	3.0	.	21.9	21.9	22.2	17.1	.	.
Guatemala	2.0	2.0	1.6	1.8	1.8	.	22.3	19.5	15.7	13.7	12.4	.
Haiti	.	.	.	1.5	1.2	1.9	.	.	.	14.9	16.5	20.6
Honduras	2.9	3.1	3.7	3.2	4.4	4.9	27.2	18.4	20.3	14.2	13.8	19.5
Jamaica	3.3	3.5	5.9	6.9	5.7	5.2	16.4	.	16.0	13.1	12.1	11.0
Mexico	2.4	2.6	3.6	4.2	3.9	3.4	8.2	8.5	11.9	.	.	.
Nicaragua	1.9	2.3	2.4	3.2	6.1	6.2	17.4	18.1	13.1	10.4	10.2	12.0
Panama	4.1	5.4	5.7	5.0	5.2	5.4	.	22.1	21.3	19.0	18.7	14.3
Paraguay	1.9	2.2	1.6	1.5	1.5	.	.	15.3	14.0	16.4	16.7	.
Peru	5.1	3.8	3.3	3.1	2.7	3.3	18.1	8.8	16.6	15.2	15.7	.
Trinidad & Tobago	3.5	3.9	3.1	4.0	5.8	.	14.1	14.0	14.7	11.5	.	.
Uruguay	3.7	3.6	.	2.2	2.6	3.1	.	26.1	.	10.0	9.3	15.0

Table A-4. Government Spending on Education (continued)

	Total central government spending on education											
	as a % of GNP						as a % of total government exp.					
	1965	1970	1975	1980	1985	1987	1965	1970	1975	1980	1985	1987
Latin America (cont.):												
Venezuela	.	.	4.5	4.4	5.4	.	18.0	22.9	.	14.7	21.3	.
Middle East (17):												
Algeria	4.0	5.9	6.7	7.8	8.6	9.8	14.8	22.4	23.0	24.3	24.3	27.8
Bahrain	.	5.8	.	2.8	3.8	5.0	22.4	20.0	8.8	10.3	.	.
Egypt	4.8	4.8	5.1	5.7	6.3	5.5	12.9	15.8	.	9.4	.	.
Iran	3.2	2.9	.	7.2	.	.	14.6	8.6	.	15.7	17.2	18.1
Iraq	.	.	.	2.6	3.8	.	23.1	19.8	6.9	.	6.5	6.4
Jordan	3.0	3.9	5.1	6.5	6.9	4.9	9.2	9.3	8.1	11.3	13.0	7.6
Kuwait	3.0	4.5	3.0	2.4	4.5	5.3	6.9	11.2	10.0	8.1	9.5	.
Lebanon	.	.	.	.	.	.	15.5	16.8	16.1	13.2	16.8	.
Morocco	3.8	4.2	5.1	6.4	8.0	8.3	.	16.8	14.3	18.5	26.7	25.5
Oman	.	1.3	1.6	2.1	4.0	4.0	.	2.8	1.9	4.1	.	15.0
Saudi Arabia	.	.	10.3	5.4	7.5	.	13.0	9.8	11.7	8.7	9.1	13.6
Syria	2.9	4.0	3.9	4.6	6.1	4.7	12.4	9.4	7.8	8.1	11.8	14.0
Tunisia	4.0	7.0	5.2	5.4	5.9	6.3	24.4	23.2	16.4	16.4	.	.
Turkey	3.7	2.9	.	2.8	2.3	1.7	19.4	13.7	.	10.5	.	.
U. Arab Emirates	.	.	0.9	1.3	1.7	2.0	.	.	.	.	10.4	13.2
Yemen, A.R.	.	0.4	.	7.4	5.4	5.0	5.1	5.9	.	.	.	.
Yemen, P.D.R.	.	.	4.0	6.2	.	.	14.1	10.9	.			

Source: UNESCO data; see technical note for full reference.

Table A-5. Per Capita Gross National Income

	in constant 1980 US dollars					
	1968	*1970*	*1975*	*1980*	*1985*	*1987*
Africa (31):						
Benin	350	350	310	330	340	320
Botswana	310	370	570	940	1,030	1,050
Burkina Faso	180	180	180	180	200	210
Burundi	140	180	190	220	250	240
Cameroon	540	580	570	780	1,060	920
Central African R.	370	390	330	350	330	320
Chad	250	260	240	160	190	160
Côte d'Ivoire	910	970	1,090	1,200	1,010	930
Ethiopia	100	110	110	110	100	100
Ghana	420	470	410	410	340	350
Kenya	330	330	370	410	340	380
Lesotho	210	240	380	480	.	370
Madagascar	460	490	420	370	290	270
Malawi	150	160	210	190	180	170
Mali	210	210	210	250	240	270
Mauritania	480	490	500	430	450	470
Mauritius	700	770	1,350	1,160	1,280	1,770
Mozambique	.	.	.	200	120	110
Niger	530	490	330	450	370	360
Nigeria	530	770	1,050	1,170	910	790
Rwanda	180	200	180	230	230	220
Senegal	580	570	570	510	510	530
Sierra Leone	250	320	300	330	300	270
Somalia	130	120	130	140	140	140
Sudan	350	340	350	360	310	360
Tanzania	320	330	310	270	230	220
Togo	330	350	360	430	320	310
Uganda	220	240	180	140	.	260
Zaire	500	530	460	380	300	210
Zambia	1,310	1,390	760	640	500	460
Zimbabwe	.	.	.	750	750	660
Asia (15):						
Bangladesh	160	160	130	150	150	160
Bhutan	.	.	.	.	.	150
China	150	210	240	300	450	510
India	230	240	240	250	300	310
Indonesia	220	240	330	500	560	560
Korea, Rep.	760	890	1,210	1,590	2,230	2,900
Lao, PDR	.	.	.	.	.	170
Malaysia	860	930	1,100	1,720	1,780	1,700
Nepal	.	.	.	.	.	160
Pakistan	230	260	240	280	320	340
Papua New G.	730	820	800	800	680	700
Philippines	500	530	610	710	580	620
Singapore	.					
Sri Lanka	200	210	210	270	330	330
Thailand	460	500	530	680	760	830
Latin America (21):						
Argentina	1,640	1,810	1,930	1,990	1,570	1,650
Bolivia	420	450	520	520	390	350
Brazil	970	1,130	1,610	1,910	1,740	1,930
Chile	2,370	2,460	1,760	2,400	1,940	2,180
Colombia	790	880	1,050	1,290	1,270	1,360
Costa Rica	1,510	1,650	1,790	2,070	1,830	2,030
Dominican Rep.	640	760	1,090	1,170	980	1,040
Ecuador	740	790	1,060	1,370	1,200	1,030
El Salvador	670	730	770	780	610	600
Guatemala	870	930	990	1,130	900	880
Haiti	210	210	220	270	230	230
Honduras	550	520	520	650	540	540
Jamaica	1,320	1,520	1,680	1,140	990	940
Mexico	1,660	1,880	2,200	2,690	2,480	1,130
Nicaragua	970	950	970	740	550	490
Panama	1,290	1,430	1,590	1,700	1,770	1,830
Paraguay	760	790	960	1,470	1,300	1,240
Peru	1,010	1,070	1,120	1,140	920	1,070
Trinidad & Tobago	1,890	1,860	3,470	5,410	3,380	1,880
Uruguay	2,460	2,770	2,860	3,480	2,680	3,220
Venezuela	.	.	4,120	4,640	3,720	3,390

Table A-5. Per Capita Gross National Income (continued)

	in 1980 constant US dollars					
	1968	*1970*	*1975*	*1980*	*1985*	*1987*
Middle East (13):						
Algeria	850	980	1,580	2,200	2,480	2,040
Egypt	320	350	360	520	590	540
Jordan	.	1,030	1,010	1,500	1,560	1,580
Kuwait	.	.	.	.	.	14,610
Morocco	660	710	820	940	930	980
Oman	.	.	.	5,420	8,780	6,710
Saudi Arabia	.	.	.	.	.	6,200
Syria	590	610	1,270	1,490	1,440	1,160
Tunisia	730	790	1,100	1,330	1,390	1,310
Turkey	960	1,020	1,250	1,240	1,380	1,580
U.A.E.	.	.	.	.	.	15,830
Yemen, AR	.	220	330	500	560	580
Yemen, PDR	.	.	.	.	.	420

Source: World Bank data; see Technical Note for full reference.

ANNEX B: FEMALE SHARE OF PRIMARY AND SECONDARY ENROLLMENTS: A TIME SERIES

Figure B-1: Female Share of Primary & Secondary Enrollments,1965-1987

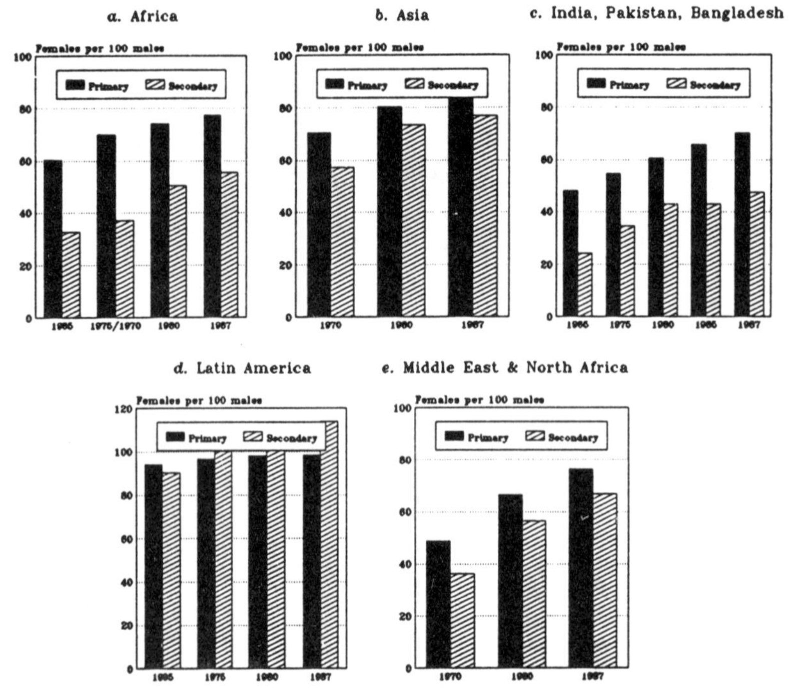

To have a more continuous time series, we amended the data set for each region to include only countries reporting data for each of the years selected. The years selected were those that would yield the maximum number of countries in each set based on the availability of male and female enrollment rates. The countries included in each regional sample are listed below. More detailed data for all countries can be found in Annex A.

a. Africa (females per 100 males)

	1965	1970	1975	1980	1987
Primary	60.4	..	70.1	74.1	75.5
Secondary	32.5	37.0	..	50.2	55.4

Primary (25): Benin, Botswana, Burkina Faso, Burundi, Cameroon, Central African Rep., Ethiopia, Guinea, Ghana, Kenya, Lesotho, Madagascar, Mauritania, Mauritius, Niger, Rwanda, Senegal, Sierra Leone, Sudan, Tanzania, Togo, Uganda, Zaire, Zambia.
Secondary (19): the same as above, less Botswana, Lesotho, Madagascar, Niger, Sierra Leone, Togo, and Zambia -- with Cote d'Ivoire added.

b. Asia (females per 100 males)

	1970	1980	1987
Primary	70.5	80.4	84.4
Secondary	57.3	73.4	76.9

Primary (12): Bangladesh, Hong Kong, India, Indonesia, Korea Rep., Lao P.D.R, Malaysia, Nepal, Pakistan, Papua New Guinea, Singapore, Sri Lanka.
Secondary (10): the same as above, less Bangladesh and Indonesia.

***c.* India, Pakistan, and Bangladesh (females per 100 males)**

	1965	1975	1980	1985	1987
Primary	48.1	54.7	60.6	65.9	70.3
Secondary	24.2	34.6	42.8	42.8	47.4

***d.* Latin America (females per 100 males)**

	1965	1975	1980	1987
Primary	94.0	96.7	98.3	98.6
Secondary	90.0	100.1	105.0	113.7

Primary (16): Argentina, Bolivia, Chile, Colombia, Costa Rica, Ecuador, El Salvador, Guatemala, Honduras, Jamaica, Mexico, Nicaragua, Panama, Paraguay, Trinidad and Tobago, Uruguay
Secondary (13): the same as above, less Argentina, Bolivia, Guatemala, Honduras, Nicaragua, Paraguay -- with Brazil, Haiti, and Peru added.

***e.* Middle East (females per 100 males)**

	1970	1980	1987
Primary	48.8	66.6	76.5
Secondary	36.3	56.4	66.9

Primary (14): Afghanistan, Algeria, Egypt, Iraq, Kuwait, Morocco, Oman, Saudi Arabia, Syria, Tunisia, Turkey, United Arab Emirates, Yemen AR, Yemen PDR.
Secondary (13): the same as above, less Oman.

ANNEX C: TRANSITION MATRICES

The following matrices (Tables C-1 and C-2) were developed as a means of presenting, in two dimensions, two issues: level of average enrollment and gender equity in enrollment, and the transitions that countries make with respect to these two dimensions (enrollment and equity). For level of average enrollment the matrices have been designed to separate countries with high, medium and low enrollment rates as follows: high, >75% for primary and >30% for secondary; medium, 45-75% for primary and 16-30% for secondary; and low, <45% for primary and <15% for secondary. Similarly for gender parity the matrices have been designed to categorize countries with the same level of average enrollment according to the degree of gender parity they have achieved. Countries again fall broadly into three groups: those with a high gender parity (female/male ratio >75%); medium gender parity (female/male ratio 45-75%); and low gender parity (female/male ratio <45%).

The progress countries have made in improving total average enrollment and gender parity of enrollment are shown separately for each region, and for primary and secondary enrollments. Within each cell in the matrices the countries are ranked from highest to lowest equity ratio.

Table C-1: Transition Matrix for Changes in Primary Enrollment and Gender Parity (1965–87)

Gender Ratio (females per 100 males)	Total average enrollment rates, 1965 (LOW) 1 - 15%	Total average enrollment rates, 1965 (MEDIUM) 16 - 30%	Total average enrollment rates, 1965 (HIGH) > 30%	Total average enrollment rates, 1987 (LOW) 1 - 15%	Total average enrollment rates, 1987 (MEDIUM) 16 - 30%	Total average enrollment rates, 1987 (HIGH) > 30%
Africa (n = 32)						
(HIGH) > 75		Botswana Madagascar Zambia	Lesotho Mauritius		Tanzania Rwanda Uganda Malawi Ghana Nigeria Mozambique	Lesotho Botswana Mauritius Zimbabwe Kenya Madagascar Zambia Cameroon Zaire
(MED.) 45 - 75	Tanzania Nigeria Malawi Sierra Leone Sudan Senegal Mozambique Mali Burkina Faso Niger Benin	Ghana Rwanda Uganda Kenya Cote d'Ivoire Zaire	Zimbabwe Cameroon	Ethiopia Mali Burkina Faso Niger Somalia	Burundi Sierra Leone Sudan Senegal Mauritania C.A.R. Liberia Benin	Cote d'Ivoire Togo
(LOW) < 45	Burundi Liberia Ethiopia Mauritania Somalia Chad	Togo C.A.R.			Chad	
Asia (n = 12)						
(HIGH) > 75		Indonesia	Philippines Korea Sri Lanka Malaysia		Papua New Guinea Bangladesh	Philippines Korea Malaysia Sri Lanka Indonesia Lao PDR
(MED.) 45 - 75	Papua New Guinea Lao PDR	India Bangladesh		Bhutan Pakistan		India Nepal
(LOW) < 45	Pakistan Nepal Bhutan					
The Middle East and North Africa (n = 15)						
(HIGH) > 75			Kuwait Jordan Lebanon			Jordan Kuwait Turkey Lebanon Syria Iraq Iran Tunisia Saudi Arabia Algeria Egypt
(MED.) 45 - 75		Egypt Algeria Iran	Turkey Tunisia Syria	Afganistan	Morocco	
(LOW) < 45	Saudi Arabia Yemen, PDR Afghanistan Yemen, AR	Iraq Morocco			Yemen, PDR	Yemen, Arab Rep.

Table C-2: Transition Matrix for Changes in Secondary Enrollment and Gender Parity (1965–87)

Gender Ratio (females per 100 males)	Total average enrollment rates, 1965 (LOW) 1 - 15%	Total average enrollment rates, 1965 (MEDIUM) 16 - 30%	Total average enrollment rates, 1965 (HIGH) > 30%	Total average enrollment rates, 1987 (LOW) 1 - 15%	Total average enrollment rates, 1987 (MEDIUM) 16 - 30%	Total average enrollment rates, 1987 (HIGH) > 30%
Africa (n = 32)						
(HIGH) > 75	Lesotho				Lesotho Madagascar	Botswana Mauritius Zimbabwe
(MED.) 45 - 75	Mozambique Zimbabwe Botswana Burundi Mali Burkina Faso	Mauritius		Rwanda Ethiopia Tanzania Malawi Mozambique Uganda Burkina Faso Burundi Somalia	Kenya Cameroon Sudan Nigeria Zambia Sierra Leone Sengal Cote d'Ivoire	Ghana
(LOW) < 45	Nigeria Benin Madagascar Sierra Leone Liberia Ghana Tanzania Malawi Rwanda Ethiopia Kenya Uganda Senegal Zambia Sudan Zaire Somalia C.A.R. Cameroon Togo Cote d'Ivoire Mauritania Niger Chad			Mali C.A.R. Niger Chad	Zaire Liberia Maurtania Benin Togo	
Asia (n = 13)						
(HIGH) > 75			Philippines Sri Lanka		Thailand	Korea Sri Lanka Philippines Malaysia
(MED.) 45 - 75	Thailand Lao, PDR	Malaysia	Korea	Papua New Guinea	Lao, PDR Bangladesh	Indonesia India
(LOW) < 45	Indonesia Pakistan Nepal Bangladesh Papua New Guinea Bhutan	India		Bhutan	Pakistan Nepal	
The Middle East and North Africa (n = 15)						
(HIGH) > 75						Lebanon Jordan Kuwait Algeria
(MED.) 45 - 75	Algeria	Lebanon Iran	Kuwait	Afghanistan		Egypt Syria Tunisia Morocco Iran Saudi Arabia Iraq Turkey
(LOW) < 45	Morocco Yemen, PDR Afghanistan Saudi Arabia Yemen, Arab Rep.	Turkey Egypt Tunisia Iraq Syria	Jordan		Yemen, PDR Yemen, Arab Rep.	

Source: see Annex C

One conventional notion about progress in girl's education is that if per capita income is higher, or growing at a good rate, average enrollments will increase and the gender gap will take care of itself. Countries can be categorized by their transition performance (best, good, and worst -- best being those that attain high average enrollment and high gender parity) in the preceeding tables. The following tables (C-3, C-4 and C-5) show the distribution of countries according to per capita income and public spending.

As with the Time Series exercise in Annex B, there is some attrition of the data set based on the availability of enrollment rate data for both 1965 and 1987. The number of countries included in the final matrices is further affected by gaps in per capita income or data on public spending.

Table C-3: Relative Per Capita Income (1987) and Equity in Educational Growth (1965-87)

a. Primary Enrollment

Performance: Enrollment & Equity	Per Capita Income, 1987 (in 1980 dollars) (n = 41)										
	< 200	200 - 299	300 - 399	400 - 499	500 - 599	600 - 699	700 - 899	900 - 1,199	1,200 - 1,599	1,600-2,000	>2,000
Best	Lao, PDR	Madagascar	Sri Lanka Lesotho Kenya	Zambia	Egypt Indonesia	Zimbabwe Philippines		Botswana Cameroon Syria	Tunisia Jordan Turkey	Malaysia Mauritius	Korea Kuwait Algeria Saudi Arabia
Good	Malawi Mozambique Bangladesh	Uganda Tanzania Rwanda	Ghana				Papua N.G. Nigeria	Morocco			
Worst	Bhutan Burkina Faso Chad Ethiopia	Mali	Pakistan Niger	Yemen, PDR	Yemen, AR						

b. Secondary Enrollment

Performance: Enrollment & Equity	Per Capita Income, 1987 (in 1980 dollars) (n = 35)										
	< 200	200 - 299	300 - 399	400 - 499	500 - 599	600 - 699	700 - 899	900 - 1,199	1,200 - 1,599	1,600-2,000	>2,000
Best			Sri Lanka			Zimbabwe Philippines		Botswana	Jordan	Malaysia Mauritius	Korea Algeria
Good	Bangladesh	Madagascar	Lesotho India		Indonesia Egypt		Papua N.G. Thailand	Morocco Syria	Turkey Tunisia		
Worst	Chad Nepal Bhutan	Mali Zaire	Benin C.A.R. Pakistan Niger Togo	Mauritania Yemen, PDR	Yemen, AR		Nigeria				

Table C-4: Real Growth in Per Capita Income (%) and Equity in Educational Growth (1965–87)

a. Primary Enrollment

Performance: Enrollment & Equity	Percent Change in Per Capita Income (in 1980 dollars), 1968 - 87 (n = 34)								
	<-50%	-50% - 0%	1% - 20%	21% - 40%	41% - 70%	71% - 100%	101% - 200%	201% - 300%	>300%
Best	Zambia - 65 Zaire - 58	Madagascar - 41	Kenya 15	Philippines 24	Sri Lanka 65 Egypt 69 Cameroon 70 Turkey 65	Lesotho 76 Tunisia 90 Syria 97 Malaysia 98	Indonesia 155 Mauritius 153 Algeria 140	Botswana 239 Korea 282	
Good		Paupa N.G. -4 Bangladesh 0 Tanzania -31 Ghana -17	Malawi 13 Uganda 18	Rwanda 22	Nigeria 49 Morocco 49				
Worst		Chad -36 Ethiopia 0 Niger -32	Burkina Faso 17 Somalia 8	Mali 29	Pakistan 48				

b. Secondary Enrollment

Performance: Enrollment & Equity	Percent Change in Per Capita Income (in 1980 dollars), 1968 - 87 (n = 28)								
	<-30%	-30% - 0%	1% - 20%	21% - 40%	41% - 70%	71% - 100%	101% - 200%	201% - 300%	>300%
Best				Philippines 24	Sri Lanka 65	Malaysia 97	Algeria 140 Mauritius 153	Korea 282 Botswana 239	
Good	Madagascar -41	Ghana -17		India 32	Morocco 49 Egypt 69 Turkey 65	Lesotho 76 Thailand 80 Tunisia 90 Syria 97	Indonesia 155	China 240	
Worst	Zaire -58 Chad -36 Niger -32	Mauritania -2 Togo -6 Benin -7 C.A.R. -14		Mali 29	Pakistan 48				

Table C-5: Government Spending on Education and Equity in Growth: Secondary Enrollment (1965–87)

a. Spending on Education as a Percent of Per Capita GNP

Enrollment & Equity Performance	Percent of Per Capita GNP, 1975, 1980, 1985 averaged (n = 31)								
	< 1%	1% - 1.9%	2% - 2.9%	3% - 3.9%	4% - 4.9%	5% - 5.9%	6% - 6.9%	7% - 7.9%	8% +
Best6p2A		Philippines 1.3		Sri Lanka 3.0 Korea 3.6 Kuwait 3.3	Mauritius 4.2		Zimbabwe 6.2 Jordan 6.2 Malaysia 6.2	Botswana 7.8 Algeria 7.7	
Good			Indonesia 2.2 Turkey 2.6 Oman 2.6	Ghana 3.9 India 3.0	Syria 4.9 Lesotho 4.4 Madagascar 4.0	Egypt 5.7 Tunisia 5.5	Morocco 6.5	Iran 7.2	
Worst			Niger 2.8 Pakistan 2.1 Nepal 2.0	Mauritania 3.8 C.A.R. 3.8 Liberia 3.8 Mali 3.7	Togo 4.8		Yemen, AR 6.4		

b. Spending on Education as a Percent of Total Government Spending

Enrollment & Equity Performance	Percent of Government Spending, 1975, 1980 & 1985 averaged (n = 31)						
	< 5%	5% - 9%	10% - 14%	15% - 19%	20% - 24%	25% - 29%	30% +
Best		Philippines Sri Lanka	Mauritius Zimbabwe Jordan	Malaysia Botswana	Korea	Algeria	
Good		India Thailand Syria Egypt	Bangladesh Indonesia Zambia Turkey	Kenya Cote d'Ivoire Lesotho Madagascar Tunisia Morocco	Cameroon Ghana	Morocco	
Worst		Pakistan	Nepal	Togo	C.A.R. Niger		

Distributors of World Bank Publications

ARGENTINA
Carlos Hirsch, SRL
Galeria Guemes
Florida 165, 4th Floor-Ofc. 453/465
1333 Buenos Aires

AUSTRALIA, PAPUA NEW GUINEA, FIJI, SOLOMON ISLANDS, VANUATU, AND WESTERN SAMOA
D.A. Books & Journals
648 Whitehorse Road
Mitcham 3132
Victoria

AUSTRIA
Gerold and Co.
Graben 31
A-1011 Wien

BAHRAIN
Bahrain Research and Consultancy Associates Ltd.
P.O. Box 22103
Manama Town 317

BANGLADESH
Micro Industries Development Assistance Society (MIDAS)
House 5, Road 16
Dhanmondi R/Area
Dhaka 1209

Branch offices:
Main Road
Maijdee Court
Noakhali - 3800

76, K.D.A. Avenue
Kulna

BELGIUM
Jean De Lannoy
Av. du Roi 202
1060 Brussels

CANADA
Le Diffuseur
C.P. 85, 1501B rue Ampère
Boucherville, Québec
J4B 5E6

CHINA
China Financial & Economic Publishing House
8, Da Fo Si Dong Jie
Beijing

COLOMBIA
Infoenlace Ltda.
Apartado Aereo 34270
Bogota D.E.

COTE D'IVOIRE
Centre d'Edition et de Diffusion Africaines (CEDA)
04 B.P. 541
Abidjan 04 Plateau

CYPRUS
MEMRB Information Services
P.O. Box 2098
Nicosia

DENMARK
SamfundsLitteratur
Rosenoerns Allé 11
DK-1970 Frederiksberg C

DOMINICAN REPUBLIC
Editora Taller, C. por A.
Restauración e Isabel la Católica 309
Apartado Postal 2190
Santo Domingo

EL SALVADOR
Fusades
Avenida Manuel Enrique Araujo #3530
Edificio SISA, ler. Piso
San Salvador

EGYPT, ARAB REPUBLIC OF
Al Ahram
Al Galaa Street
Cairo

The Middle East Observer
8 Chawarbi Street
Cairo

FINLAND
Akateeminen Kirjakauppa
P.O. Box 128
SF-00101
Helsinki 10

FRANCE
World Bank Publications
66, avenue d'Iéna
75116 Paris

GERMANY
UNO-Verlag
Poppelsdorfer Allee 55
D-5300 Bonn 1

GREECE
KEME
24, Ippodamou Street Platia Plastiras
Athens-11635

GUATEMALA
Librerias Piedra Santa
5a. Calle 7-55
Zona 1
Guatemala City

HONG KONG, MACAO
Asia 2000 Ltd.
6 Fl., 146 Prince Edward Road, W.
Kowloon
Hong Kong

INDIA
Allied Publishers Private Ltd.
751 Mount Road
Madras - 600 002

Branch offices:
15 J.N. Heredia Marg
Ballard Estate
Bombay - 400 038

13/14 Asaf Ali Road
New Delhi - 110 002

17 Chittaranjan Avenue
Calcutta - 700 072

Jayadeva Hostel Building
5th Main Road Gandhinagar
Bangalore - 560 009

3-5-1129 Kachiguda Cross Road
Hyderabad - 500 027

Prarthana Flats, 2nd Floor
Near Thakore Baug, Navrangpura
Ahmedabad - 380 009

Patiala House
16-A Ashok Marg
Lucknow - 226 001

INDONESIA
Pt. Indira Limited
Jl. Sam Ratulangi 37
P.O. Box 181
Jakarta Pusat

ITALY
Licosa Commissionaria Sansoni SPA
Via Benedetto Fortini, 120/10
Casella Postale 552
50125 Florence

JAPAN
Eastern Book Service
37-3, Hongo 3-Chome, Bunkyo-ku 113
Tokyo

KENYA
Africa Book Service (E.A.) Ltd.
P.O. Box 45245
Nairobi

KOREA, REPUBLIC OF
Pan Korea Book Corporation
P.O. Box 101, Kwangwhamun
Seoul

KUWAIT
MEMRB Information Services
P.O. Box 5465

MALAYSIA
University of Malaya Cooperative Bookshop, Limited
P.O. Box 1127, Jalan Pantai Baru
Kuala Lumpur

MEXICO
INFOTEC
Apartado Postal 22-860
14060 Tlalpan, Mexico D.F.

MOROCCO
Société d'Etudes Marketing Marocaine
12 rue Mozart, Bd. d'Anfa
Casablanca

NETHERLANDS
InOr-Publikaties b.v.
P.O. Box 14
7240 BA Lochem

NEW ZEALAND
Hills Library and Information Service
Private Bag
New Market
Auckland

NIGERIA
University Press Limited
Three Crowns Building Jericho
Private Mail Bag 5095
Ibadan

NORWAY
Narvesen Information Center
Book Department
P.O. Box 6125 Etterstad
N-0602 Oslo 6

OMAN
MEMRB Information Services
P.O. Box 1613, Seeb Airport
Muscat

PAKISTAN
Mirza Book Agency
65, Shahrah-e-Quaid-e-Azam
P.O. Box No. 729
Lahore 3

PERU
Editorial Desarrollo SA
Apartado 3824
Lima

PHILIPPINES
International Book Center
Fifth Floor, Filipinas Life Building
Ayala Avenue, Makati
Metro Manila

POLAND
ORPAN
Palac Kultury i Nauki
00-901 Warszawa

PORTUGAL
Livraria Portugal
Rua Do Carmo 70-74
1200 Lisbon

SAUDI ARABIA, QATAR
Jarir Book Store
P.O. Box 3196
Riyadh 11471

MEMRB Information Services
Branch offices:
Al Alsa Street
Al Dahna Center
First Floor
P.O. Box 7188
Riyadh

Haji Abdullah Alireza Building
King Khaled Street
P.O. Box 3969
Damman

33, Mohammed Hassan Awad Street
P.O. Box 5978
Jeddah

SINGAPORE, TAIWAN, MYANMAR, BRUNEI
Information Publications Private, Ltd.
02-06 1st Fl., Pei-Fu Industrial Bldg.
24 New Industrial Road
Singapore 1953

SOUTH AFRICA, BOTSWANA
For single titles:
Oxford University Press Southern Africa
P.O. Box 1141
Cape Town 8000

For subscription orders:
International Subscription Service
P.O. Box 41095
Craighall
Johannesburg 2024

SPAIN
Mundi-Prensa Libros, S.A.
Castello 37
28001 Madrid

Libreria Internacional AEDOS
Consell de Cent, 391
08009 Barcelona

SRI LANKA AND THE MALDIVES
Lake House Bookshop
P.O. Box 244
100, Sir Chittampalam A. Gardiner Mawatha
Colombo 2

SWEDEN
For single titles:
Fritzes Fackboksforetaget
Regeringsgatan 12, Box 16356
S-103 27 Stockholm

For subscription orders:
Wennergren-Williams AB
Box 30004
S-104 25 Stockholm

SWITZERLAND
For single titles:
Librairie Payot
6, rue Grenus
Case postale 381
CH 1211 Geneva 11

For subscription orders:
Librairie Payot
Service des Abonnements
Case postale 3312
CH 1002 Lausanne

TANZANIA
Oxford University Press
P.O. Box 5299
Dar es Salaam

THAILAND
Central Department Store
306 Silom Road
Bangkok

TRINIDAD & TOBAGO, ANTIGUA BARBUDA, BARBADOS, DOMINICA, GRENADA, GUYANA, JAMAICA, MONTSERRAT, ST. KITTS & NEVIS, ST. LUCIA, ST. VINCENT & GRENADINES
Systematics Studies Unit
#9 Watts Street
Curepe
Trinidad, West Indies

UNITED ARAB EMIRATES
MEMRB Gulf Co.
P.O. Box 6097
Sharjah

UNITED KINGDOM
Microinfo Ltd.
P.O. Box 3
Alton, Hampshire GU34 2PG
England

VENEZUELA
Libreria del Este
Aptdo. 60.337
Caracas 1060-A

YUGOSLAVIA
Jugoslovenska Knjiga
P.O. Box 36
Trg Republike
YU-11000 Belgrade